PAUL THE LEADER

Paul the Leader

J. OSWALD SANDERS

STL BOOKS
BROMLEY
KINGSWAY PUBLICATIONS
EASTBOURNE

Unless otherwise indicated, biblical quotations
are from the New International Version,
© New York International Bible Society 1978

NEB = New English Bible
© Delegates of the Oxford University Press and
Syndics of the Cambridge University Press 1961, 1970

TLB = The Living Bible
© Tyndale House Publishers 1971

ISBN 0 86065 219 X (Kingsway)
ISBN 0 903843 74 9 (STL)

STL Books are published by
Send the Light (Operation Mobilisation)
P.O. Box 48, Bromley,
Kent, England.

KINGSWAY PUBLICATIONS LTD
Lottbridge Drove, Eastbourne, E. Sussex BN23 6NT.
Typeset by Nuprint Services Ltd, Harpenden, Herts.
Printed and bound in Great Britain
by Collins, Glasgow.

Contents

Preface

This volume is the outcome of a request that I follow up my former book, *Spiritual Leadership*, with another in which the leadership principles there enunciated are illustrated from the life and ministry of Paul the Apostle.

I realize that many more important works on Paul have come from more able pens, but I have not as yet found one that specifically treats Paul's life from this angle. The fact that many have expressed the opinion that a book of this nature would meet a need has encouraged me to make the attempt.

In its preparation I acknowledge especial indebtedness to a small volume published at the beginning of the century—*The Man Paul* by Robert E. Speer, Secretary of the American Presbyterian Board of Foreign Missions. It is an extremely perceptive and valuable study of the Apostle. I have followed his example in including some apposite verses from F. W. H. Myers' magnificent poem, *Saint Paul.*[1]

It is my hope that the book may prove helpful in Bible study and home groups. With this in view I have included numerous Scripture references. Unless otherwise stated, the quotations are from the New International Version

J. Oswald Sanders

1

A Man Just Like us

The strong, sure, charismatic leadership so desperately needed in our confused age seems to be conspicuously lacking. One concerned citizen, disturbed by prevailing conditions and the inability of his nation's leaders to find a panacea for their ills, made this comment:

> The critical juncture found none but second-rate actors on the political stage, and the decisive moment was neglected because the courageous were deficient in power, and the powerful in sagacity, courage and resolution.[2]

That sounds strangely contemporary, yet it was written a century ago by Friedrich Stiller. Have things changed essentially in the intervening years? Our Lord's graphic words are proving true, and accurately diagnose conditions today: 'On the earth, nations will be in anguish and perplexity at the roaring and the tossing of the sea' (Lk 21:25).

World conditions may have worsened immeasurably since then, but the same appraisal of the situation would be appropriate. Each generation has to meet and resolve its own leadership problems, and today we are facing an acute crisis in leadership in many spheres. Crisis succeeds crisis, yet our leaders come up with few solutions, and the prognosis is by no means reassuring.

The Church has not escaped this dearth of authoritative leadership. The voice that once sounded a clarion call of hope to beleaguered humanity is now strangely muted, and the influence of the Church in the world community has become minimal. The salt has largely lost its savour, and the light its radiance.

Merely to bemoan this state of affairs is counter-productive. A more constructive approach would be to discover afresh the principles and factors that inspired the dynamic spiritual leadership of Paul and the other apostles in the halcyon days of the Church. And not only to discover them, but to endeavour to apply them to our own situation. Spiritual principles are timeless— they do not change from generation to generation.

A friend once remarked to the author: 'Isn't it a humbling thing to see one's own faults running around on two little legs!' When we see them embodied in someone else, our faults become painfully obvious to us. Similarly, we can grasp spiritual principles more readily when we see them embodied in a person than when formulated as mere academic propositions.

This is why one of the most rewarding Bible studies is to trace the interplay of divine providence and human personality in the lives of men and women just like us; to discover how the conditions and experiences of early life had been controlled and shaped by a skilful and beneficent Hand.

We must be grateful that divine inspiration has ensured the preservation and selection of the providential factors involved. The plain, unvarnished facts are recorded in a straightforward manner, and with no attempt to retouch the photograph. The Bible is careful to portray its characters as they really were, 'warts and all'.

It is in our Lord and not in Paul that we see the ideal of leadership, for He is the Leader *par excellence*. There are some, however, who find His very perfection daunting and rather discouraging. Because He inherited no sinful nature as we do, they feel that this fact conferred on Him a vast advantage, and removed Him from the arena of their earthy struggles and failures. He seems so far above them that they are able to draw very little practical help from His shining example. While this viewpoint springs from a misconception of the nature of the help Christ is able to extend, its results are very real.

In the Apostle Paul God has provided the example of '*a man just like us*' (Jas 5:17). True he was a man of towering stature, but he was also a man who knew failure as well as success; a man who cried in despair: 'What a wretched man I am! Who will rescue me from this body of death?', and yet who exulted, 'Thanks be to God—through Jesus Christ our Lord' (Rom 7:24, 25).

These and similar outpourings of his heart bring him into our street, where we can more easily identify with his experiences. He was not 'an impossible saint', but a frail, fallible man just like us, who can speak to our need.

So, in Christ we have the inspiration of a real Man who never failed, while in Paul we have the encouragement of a man who fell and rose again. 'A perfect man reveals what the ideal is, a man defeated and finally victorious discloses what by the grace of God we may become . . . We need Jesus on one side of us and Paul on the other if we are to walk in triumph along the difficult and perilous way.'[3]

If our study of Paul's leadership principles is to be permanently fruitful, it must be more than academic. Each reader in his own life and sphere of service will need to master and translate them into action. The facts must become factors of experience.

We should be grateful to him for the unconscious self-revelation that characterizes his letters. We learn far more about him from his own indirect and unstudied references in his letters than we do from Luke's historical material in the book of Acts. In his biography of the late A. W. Tozer, D. J. Fant adopted the method of interpreting the man from his own writings, and this is the method that will be followed in these studies.

In Paul we find an inspiring prototype of what one man, wholly abandoned to God, can achieve in a single generation. It will be our purpose to view him especially in his role as a leader in the Church; to consider his viewpoint on relevant subjects; to examine the qualities that made him the man he was, and to discover how these traits contributed to his superb leadership.

2

The Preparation of a Leader

From the earliest days of which we have a record, Paul displayed incipient qualities of leadership which developed with the years. While we must avoid the error of attributing to him almost superhuman qualities and sanctity, we cannot escape the conclusion that he was a man of immense stature and personality—one of those colossal figures who impress themselves indelibly on history. And yet a closer study reveals a vulnerable, lovable 'man of like passions' whose life was rendered extraordinary by a more than ordinary faith and unreserved surrender to his Master.

He has been nominated the world's most successful Christian, and his career the most astonishing in world history. Perhaps no other has attained the same heights in so many capacities. His versatility was such that in retrospect it seems as though he possessed almost every gift. But despite his awe-inspiring record, in his writings he succeeds in establishing rapport with the humble believer as easily as with the erudite philosopher.

It has been suggested that a present-day parallel to the Apostle would be a man who could speak Chinese in Peking, quoting Confucius and Mencius; write closely reasoned theology in English and expound it at Oxford; defend his cause in Russian before the Soviet Academy of Sciences.

In his book, *The Man who Shook the World,* John Pollock

tells of the impression a study of Paul's life and work made on him: 'A biographer's nose develops a sort of instinct, and it was not long before I was struck by the credibility, the genuineness of the person who was emerging from the Acts of the Apostles and the Epistles taken as a whole. A convincing character with a completely credible if astonishingly unusual story.'[4]

In autobiographical references in his letters, Paul pictures himself before his conversion as a moral, successful and law-abiding citizen. In reviewing his life at that time he saw little reason for self-reproach, and evidenced no sense of being under the disfavour of God. Indeed, if anything, he felt the reverse. He had been no prodigal. He could place his life alongside the law of God without any undue sense of having failed to meet its obligations. But his excessive zeal found unworthy expression in the ruthless persecution of followers of Christ. These qualities combined to make him one of the most difficult persons to convert to Christianity, for he was so entirely convinced of his own integrity.

His complex personality was unified, however, by a remarkable singleness of purpose. His immense intellectual powers would have made him remarkable even if he had never become a Christian. Of all the apostles, he alone was an intellectual, and this fact was to prove of great significance in the progress of the new faith. If Christianity was to make an intellectual as well as a moral and spiritual conquest of the world, it needed someone of Paul's mental calibre to explain and enforce the significance of Christ's death and resurrection and other related doctrines.

Most of the other apostles displayed some distinctive gift or trait of character, but Paul's character was so many-sided that in him they all seemed to coalesce. Peter, for example, was an extremist and Andrew a conservative. In Paul both qualities are evident. On occasion he was as venturesome and impetuous as Peter, but if necessary he could be as cautious as Andrew. He was conservative where principle was involved, while at the same time prepared to adopt radical methods to attain his end.

Where principle was clearly at stake he was inflexible and would not yield for a moment, even if the person involved was the prestigious Apostle Peter. When the vastly important issue of Christian liberty was at issue, Paul told the Galatians: 'We did not give in to them for a moment, so that the truth of the gospel might remain with you' (Gal 2:5).

Heredity and training

Heredity bears an important part in any life. In the providence of God, the preparation of a leader begins before his birth. Jeremiah recognized this sovereign activity of God when he recorded the Lord's word to him: 'Before I formed you in the womb I knew you, before you were born I set you apart; I appointed you as a prophet to the nations' (1:5). He was predestined to leadership, but he was to discover that his preparation would involve a long and sometimes painful training course. Paul too was conscious that he was the subject of a determining and beneficent will, although the path ahead unfolded only slowly before him.

> What to thee is shadow, to Him is day,
>   And the end He knoweth;
> And not on a blind and aimless way,
>   The spirit goeth.
>
> Like warp and woof, all destinies
>   Are woven fast,
> Linked in sympathy, like the keys
>   Of an organ vast.
>
> *J. G. Whittier*

It would be about AD 33 when Paul stood guard over the

clothes of the men who stoned Stephen. He was then described as 'a young man' (Acts 7:58), a term which could be applied to an age range extending from twenty years to over thirty. If, as seems most likely, he was a member of the prestigious Sanhedrin, he must then have been over thirty, the qualifying age for that body. This would mean that he was born somewhere about the same time as Jesus. In a sermon attributed to John Chrysostom it is inferred that he was born in the year 2 BC. On the supposition that he died about AD 66, he would have been about sixty-eight years old when he was executed.

As to heredity, Paul came from a moderately affluent family, for they met the property qualification required of citizens of Tarsus. His parents, who were of the tribe of Benjamin, named their son after his illustrious tribal ancestor, King Saul. Since his father was a Roman citizen, they added the Roman name, Paulus. This Roman citizenship placed him among the aristocracy of Tarsus.

As Paul's father was a strict Pharisee, he would fulfil for his son all the ceremonial requirements of the Law with meticulous care. Paul himself said that he had been trained scrupulously after the best traditions of the Pharisees. Tragically enough, this formerly Puritan-like body had by then become infected with legalism and hypocrisy.

He was obviously proud of his pedigree and attainments of which he wrote to the Philippian believers:

> If anyone else thinks he has reason to put confidence in the flesh, I have more: circumcised on the eighth day, of the people of Israel, of the tribe of Benjamin, a Hebrew of Hebrews; in regard to the law, a Pharisee; as for zeal, persecuting the church; as for legalistic righteousness, faultless' (Phil 3:4–6).

> Under Gamaliel I was thoroughly trained in the law of our fathers (Acts 22:3).

Thus all the formative years were calculated to prepare

him to be an eminent Pharisee and rabbi, like his great mentor Gamaliel.

His family would speak Greek, and he was also familiar with Aramaic (Acts 22:2). From earliest years he would be familiar with the Greek Septuagint Version of the Old Testament, large portions of which he would have had to commit to memory.

His early education would be either at home, or in a school connected with the synagogue, for his scrupulous parents would have been unlikely to entrust him to Gentile teachers.

Like all other boys of good families, he learned a trade. St Francis Xavier worked with his hands, and expressed the wish that all the brothers would do the same. Gamaliel held that learning of any kind unaccompanied by a trade ended in nothing but sin.

Paul's trade of tent-making proved a valuable asset in the years ahead. His native Tarsus abounded with mountain goats whose long hair was woven into strong outer garments or into tents made from material known as Cilician cloth. The advantage of this trade was that it could be pursued anywhere and required no costly equipment.

Paul was proud of his native city of Tarsus, describing it as 'no mean city'. It was one of the three great university cities of the Roman Empire, the others being Athens and Alexandria, and was said to surpass its rivals in intellectual eminence. Its scholarly atmosphere had doubtless already influenced the youth's eager mind.

At the age of about fifteen, Paul would have taken the journey to Jerusalem, where he may have lived with his sister (Acts 23:16). Apparently some of his relatives had embraced Christianity before he did (Rom 16:7). There he would have seen and heard the exciting sights and sounds of the temple service and would have watched with reverence the officiating priests and the ascending smoke from the sacrificial altar.

One of the many clear evidences of divine providence shaping his life was the fact that, probably through the influence of his family, he was privileged to 'sit at the feet of Gamaliel', who was called 'the Beauty of the Law'. This learned and notable rabbi was one of seven Jewish doctors of the law to whom the honoured title of 'Rabban' was given. He was of the school of Hillel, which embraced a broader and more liberal view than that of Shammai. Paul was thus exposed to a wider spectrum of teaching than would otherwise have been the case. Unlike Shammai, Gamaliel was interested in Greek literature and encouraged Jews to have friendship and social intercourse with foreigners. From him Paul would learn sincerity and honesty of judgement, and a willingness to study and use the works of Gentile authors.

It was this same Gamaliel who counselled moderation when the crowd would have killed Peter and the other apostles. 'A Pharisee named Gamaliel, a teacher of the law, who was honoured by all the people...addressed them..."In the present case I advise you: Leave these men alone! Let them go! For if their purpose or activity is of human origin, it will fail. But if it is from God, you will not be able to stop these men; you will only find yourself fighting against God."' (Acts 5:34–39).

After his training under Gamaliel, as a qualified and recognized Pharisee he returned home until he was old enough to embark on his life task.

In passing, it may be noted that since Gamaliel did not give sanction to persecuting activities, it is difficult to account for the subsequent unbridled fury of his pupil, unless it be that it was the outward expression of the fierce battle that raged within his breast. Robert Speer suggests that 'he was as much at war with himself as he was with the Christians.'[5]

Academically, Paul made spectacular progress. He surpassed his fellow-students in both academic achievement and in zeal. He was 'zealous for God', and 'more exceedingly zealous for the traditions of my fathers'. It is not difficult to imagine the fury of the Jewish authorities at the loss of his promising leadership.

As already mentioned, he was almost certainly a member of the Sanhedrin, the supreme Jewish legal and civil court. To qualify for this honour he would have been over thirty years old at the time of Stephen's death. Paul himself says he was one of the judges who voted in favour of the death of the Christians. 'On the authority of the chief priests I put many of the saints in prison, and when they were put to death, I cast my vote against them' (Acts 26:10).

In those days it was customary to marry at an early age, one of the necessary qualifications for a seat on the Sanhedrin being that one must be a married man. The reason behind this provision was that members were supposed to lean towards mercy, and a husband and father was thought more likely to possess that quality than an unmarried man. The weight of evidence would seem to be in favour of Paul having been a married man, but Scripture is silent on the subject. There is a tradition that he was a widower. It may have been that after his conversion to Christianity he was disowned and repudiated by his family.

Advantages

'And what was true in Paul's case', wrote F. B. Meyer, 'is as true for us all. A providence is shaping our ends; a plan is developing in our lives; a supremely wise and loving Being is making all things work together for good. In the sequel of our life's story we shall see that there was a meaning and necessity in all the previous incidents, save those which are the result of our own folly and sin, and that even those have been made to contribute to the final result.'[6]

The overruling hand of God in training him for leadership may be clearly discerned in the advantages Paul enjoyed as a result of both his heredity and his environment.

It is to be doubted if there was any other Christian man of the first century who united in himself most of the qualities and qualifications that would constitute him a world-citizen —a Jew living in a Greek city, and with Roman citizenship. Both by birth and training Paul possessed the tenacity of the Jew, the culture of the Greek and the practicality of the Roman, and these qualities enabled him to adapt to the polyglot peoples among whom he was to move.

These qualities also uniquely fitted him to be a world missionary leader. To a Roman citizen there was no such thing as a foreign land, so the vexed question of extra-territoriality that has plagued missionary work for so long was no problem for him. Visas and passports had not been thought of. Paul could never travel from under his own flag, and since a similar type of civilization obtained throughout the Empire there were few cultural barriers to surmount. Also there were few major social, economic or currency problems to be overcome. Greek was almost universally known, so language problems were minimal. In addition, his Roman citizenship proved a great boon to him on several occasions.

Because he had gained his theological education at the feet of Jewry's most famous Rabbi, no one could justly impugn his scholarship or extensive knowledge of the Law. Then, too, he was equally familiar with current philosophical systems, and could dispute with their proponents on their own ground. 'He spoke and disputed against the Hellenists' (Acts 9:29 RSV).

His tent-making skill relieved him of the disadvantage of being a financial burden on the emerging churches, and the pressures that financial obligations often generate were thus obviated. This afforded him a freedom in counsel or rebuke which would have been much more difficult had he been financially obligated to them.

Handicaps

Many missionary leaders today would gladly welcome many of the advantages Paul enjoyed. But these advantages were probably more than counterbalanced by other handicaps under which he and his colleagues had to work.

In *The Old Tea House,* Violet Alleyn Storey writes: '"Let those who think they are handicapped by some affliction in body or in spirit for a noble work in life remember Paul", one has said. Milton the blind who looked on Paradise! Beethoven the deaf who heard vast harmonies! Byron the lame who climbed towards Alpine skies! Who pleads a handicap, remember these."'

More often than not Paul had no suitable place in which to preach. Before long he was regarded as a dangerous trouble-maker, and the synagogues were closed to him.

In order to support himself, and sometimes others too, at times he had to toil night and day. The wonder is that he still found time for effective gospel witness.

He apparently suffered the handicap of being far from impressive physically. He wrote: 'Some say "his letters are weighty and forceful, but in person he is unimpressive"' (2 Cor 10:10).

In *The Acts of Paul and Hecla,* a novel written in the second or third century, there is the only known pen portrait of Paul. In it the apostle is described as 'small in size with meeting eyebrows, with a rather large nose, bald-headed, bow-legged, strongly built, full of grace, for at times he looked like a man and at times he had the face of an angel'.[7]

Though not cast in a herculean mould, he displayed incredible physical stamina, for throughout his ministry physical suffering and discomfort were routine.

He was apparently not an impressive orator like Apollos. 'His letters are weighty and forceful but...his speaking amounts to nothing' (2 Cor 10:10).

False teachers and legalists dogged his steps and

endeavoured to neutralize and dissipate his work. They impugned his apostleship and belittled his authority, compelling him reluctantly to defend himself and vindicate his divine appointment.

He suffered the acute pain arising from disaffection among his loved colleagues—Barnabas, Demas, Hymenaeus and Philetus, Phygelus and Hermogenes, to name a few. Such breaches of fellowship were desperately painful to his warm and generous pastor's heart. To fill his cup of bitterness, he wrote on one occasion that 'everyone in the province of Asia has deserted me, including Phygelus and Hermogenes' (2 Tim 1:15). This was a shattering blow to the hard-pressed leader. Then, too, not all his converts were steadfast, and they were a weight on his spirits.

Heart-burdens and acute physical sufferings and hardships were common; weariness and pain, hunger and thirst, cold and nakedness, scourgings and imprisonment, stoning and shipwreck, perils on land and sea were part and parcel of his missionary experience (see 2 Cor 11:23–28). He summed it up in one sentence: '...this body of ours had no rest, but we were harassed at every turn—conflicts on the outside, fears within' (2 Cor 7:5).

He worked under constant pressure, yet without being submerged by it. 'We were under great pressure, far beyond our ability to endure, so that we despaired even of life' (2 Cor 1:8). But the pressure was productive: 'But this happened that we might not rely on ourselves but on God'. In addition to all the other incidental pressures there was the over-arching burden of responsibility for the well-being of the churches he had helped to bring into existence. 'Besides everything else, I face daily the pressure of my concern for all the churches' (2 Cor 11:28).

Such an intolerable load would have crushed a lesser man, or a man who had not mastered the secret of casting his burden on the Lord on the one hand, and appropriating His more than sufficient grace on the other.

The apostle's attitude towards these handicaps was exemplary, and has much to teach all in positions of leadership. He did not passively and reluctantly endure them—he actually gloried in them and in the opportunity they afforded of proving and displaying the sufficiency of Christ and the adequacy of His grace. He had travelled a great distance along the road to spiritual maturity when he could say: 'For Christ's sake, I delight in weaknesses, in insults, in hardships, in persecutions, in difficulties. For when I am weak, then I am strong' (2 Cor 12:10). He did not consider them unmitigated evils but valued them as instruments designed to conform him to the image of Christ. Paradoxically the trials became channels of grace, and even occasions for rejoicing.

Conversion

The crucial importance to the history of the Church of Paul's conversion is attested by the fact that the Holy Spirit caused three full-length and complementary accounts of that event to be preserved in the Scriptures. In the light of his subsequent and continuing influence it is not too much to say that it was one of the epochal events of history. Only one other event is reported in fuller detail—the crucifixion of the Son of God.

It was while travelling the Damascus road on a persecuting foray that the young rabbi was suddenly stopped in his tracks. He had actively participated in the stoning of Stephen. 'When the blood of your martyr Stephen was shed,' he confessed, 'I stood there giving my approval and guarding the clothes of those who were killing him' (Acts 22:20). It may have been this evidence of his persecuting zeal that led to his election to the Sanhedrin, and later to his appointment as an inquisitor.

According to his own account, he embarked on his grisly task with fanatical intensity. 'I persecuted the followers of this Way to their death, arresting both men and women and throwing them into prison, as also the high priest and all the council can testify. I even obtained letters from them to their brothers in Damascus, and went there to bring these people as prisoners to Jerusalem to be punished' (Acts 22:4–7). He went even further: 'I tried to force them to blaspheme, in my obsession against them' (Acts 26:11).

In vivid words Paul recounted to King Agrippa the shattering and unforgettable experience that turned the persecutor into the preacher: 'About noon, O King, as I was on the road, I saw a light from heaven, brighter than the sun, blazing around me and my companions. We all fell to the ground, and I heard a voice saying to me in Aramaic, "Saul, Saul, why do you persecute me? It is hard for you to kick against the goads"' (Acts 26:13–14).

Without doubt Saul had been deeply affected by Stephen's demeanour in his martyrdom. Sir W. Ramsay's suggestion is that he was so sure that the impostor Jesus was dead, that when Stephen's vision was repeated in his own experience, the whole ground of his hostility collapsed.

What astounded Paul was that when Christ appeared to him it was not in wrath and vengeance, but in boundless, unconditional love. It was this that shattered his last opposition and melted the hardness of his intransigent heart.

One of the most exhaustive studies of this historic event was made in the last century by Lord Lyttelton, a parliamentarian whose name appeared in every major political debate in the British Parliament, and who held the office of Chancellor of the Exchequer in the Cabinet. He was a man of letters as well as a politician.[8]

In his treatise on the results of his investigation Lyttelton recounts that he and his lawyer friend, Gilbert West, were both convinced that the Bible was a fraud, and they determined to expose the fraud. Lyttelton chose the conversion of Paul, and West, the resurrection of Christ, the two crucial points of Christianity, as the subjects of their hostile research.

Each approached his study sincerely, though full of prejudice, but the result of their separate research, which extended over a considerable period, was that both were converted to faith in Christ through their very efforts to discredit the biblical record. When at last they came together, it was not to exult over the exposé of another imposture, but to rejoice with each other on their discovery that the Bible was indeed the Word of God.

In the opening paragraph of his treatise, Lyttelton wrote: 'The conversion and apostleship of Paul alone, duly considered, was of itself a demonstration sufficient to prove Christianity to be a divine revelation.' So convincing was Lyttelton's work that the famous Samuel Johnson declared it to be a treatise 'to which infidelity has never been able to fabricate a specious answer'.

Lyttelton laid down four propositions which he considered exhausted all the possibilities of the case:

1. Paul was either an impostor who said what he knew to be false, *or*
2. He was an enthusiast who imposed on himself by the force of an overheated imagination, *or*
3. He was deceived by the fraud of others, *or*
4. What he declared to be the cause of his conversion did really happen, and therefore the Christian religion is a divine revelation.

He further demonstrated from Scripture that Paul was not an impostor. What motive, he asked, could have induced him while journeying to Damascus with a heart filled with insensate hatred against the sect, to turn around and become a disciple of Christ? Motive was absent. Paul had betrayed no desire for wealth or reputation from his association with the group. Nor was he seeking power, for his whole life was marked by a complete absence of self-seeking. Nor was he motivated by a desire for the gratification of any other passion, for his writings urge the strictest morality.

On the other hand to become a Christian was to incur hatred and contempt, as well as to expose himself to danger. Would he have endured the 'loss of all things', and exulted in what he knew to be a fraud? That would be an imposture as unprofitable as it was perilous. So Lyttelton's conclusion was that the theory defeated itself.

One interesting sidelight is that Paul should have appealed to King Agrippa's personal knowledge of the truth of the story of his conversion: 'Paul replied, "What I am saying is true and reasonable. The king is familiar with these things, and I can speak freely to him. I am convinced that none of this has escaped his notice, because it was not done in a corner"' (Acts 26:25, 26).

In itself that is a remarkable proof both of the public knowledge of the fact, and the integrity of the man who could fearlessly call on the king to give testimony for him. If the story of his conversion had been fabricated for the occasion, how was it that the godly Ananias went to meet such a monster at Damascus?

From these and other arguments, Lyttelton drew two final conclusions:

1. Paul was not a cheat, telling a trumped up tale about his conversion.

2. If he were, he could not have succeeded.

Although it had been preceded by a long period of unconscious 'incubation', Paul's was undoubtedly a sudden conversion. He had been unable to banish from his mind the face of the dying martyr—'as it had been the face of an angel'.

Nor could he forget Stephen's last poignant prayer: 'Lord, do not hold this sin against them' (Acts 7:60).

The ever-active Holy Spirit had set the stage over the years for this grand confrontation and capitulation. The blinding flash found a vast amount of inflammable material in the heart of the young persecutor.

The miracle occurred in the full blaze of the noonday sun. He saw Jesus in all His Messianic glory and majesty. This was no mere vision, for he ranks it as the last appearance of the Saviour to His disciples, and places it on the same level as His appearances to the other apostles. His statement is clear and unequivocal:

He appeared to Peter, and then to the Twelve. After that, he appeared to more than five hundred of the brothers at the same time, most of whom are still living, though some have fallen asleep. Then he appeared to James, then to all the apostles, and last of all *he appeared to me also,* as to one abnormally born (1 Cor 15:4–8).

It was not an ecstasy, but a real and objective appearance of the risen and exalted Christ, clothed in His glorified humanity. Paul was immediately convinced that He was no impostor.

The whole event has been epitomized in blank verse by Amos R. Wells:

The light was brighter than the noonday sun, the flaming glory of the Holy One. It showed the Crucified, the Nazarene, splendid in majesty, benign, serene, blinding with Deity's effulgent blaze, the font of power and the home of praise. It showed, in cowering shame before them all, the cruel, persecuting heart of Saul, his bigotry, his madness, and his pride, and Stephen's martyr glory as he died. So piercing was the overpowering light, it blasted utterly all other sight, it whelmed in blackness all the world abroad, and centered vision on the Son of God. Roused by that light, Saul's conscience woke at last, shrank from the horrid turmoil of the past, and saw how all his life, by passion marred, had kicked against the pricks and found it hard. The light flames full on duty, sent a ray forth to the future's hope of brightening day. 'What shall I do, Lord?' Hear the trembling call, born of a new regenerated Saul. And then, dear sight restored, the light divine continued grandly governing to shine. It sent the apostle nobly forth again, Christ's witness to the world of groping men, till all the lands of misery and night glowed in the dawning of the heavenly light.[9]

What a different entrance into Damascus it was from what the inquisitor had envisaged! 'He fell to the ground and heard a voice say to him...Now get up and go into the city, and you will be told what you must do...Saul got up from the ground, but when he opened his eyes he could see nothing. So they led him by the hand into Damascus' (Acts 9:4–8). Paul entered Damascus a captive, chained to the chariot-wheel of his conquering Lord. All was dark without, but all was light within.

Paul's surrender to the Lordship of Christ was immediate and absolute. The moment he realized that Jesus was no impostor but the Messiah of the Jews, he knew there could be only one appropriate response. The whole story is epitomized in his first two questions: 'Who are you, Lord?' 'What shall I do, Lord?' (Acts 22:8, 10). True conversion always results in yielding to the will of God, for all saving faith involves obedience (Rom 1:5).

> The proudest heart that ever beat
>   Hath been subdued in me;
> The wildest will that ever rose
> To scorn Thy cause or aid Thy foes
>   Is quelled, my God, by Thee.

W. Hone

How amazing was the victorious strategy of God! C. E. Macartney writes: 'The bitterest foe became the greatest friend. The blasphemer became the preacher of Christ's love. The hand that wrote the indictment of the disciples of Christ when he brought them before magistrates and into prison now penned epistles of God's redeeming love. The heart that once beat with joy when Stephen sank beneath the bloody stones now rejoiced in scourgings and stoning for the sake of Christ. From this erstwhile enemy, persecutor, blasphemer came the greater part of the New Testament, the noblest statements of theology, the sweetest lyrics of Christian love.'[10]

Call

The call of God came to Paul in so clear and specific a manner that he could not mistake it. While he was lying on the ground, blinded by the heavenly light, Ananias communicated to him the message he had received from God: 'The God of our fathers has chosen you to know his will and to see the Righteous One and to hear words from his mouth. You will be his witness to all men of what you have seen and heard' (Acts 22:14, 15).

Later, when he returned to Jerusalem, he 'fell into a trance and saw the Lord speaking... Then the Lord said to me, "Go, I will send you far away to the Gentiles"' (Acts 22:17, 21). To the understandably fearful Ananias who was commissioned by God to welcome the notorious persecutor into the Christian Church, God also indicated the sphere of witness to which He had called him: 'The Lord said to Ananias, "Go! This man is my chosen instrument to carry my name before the Gentiles and their kings and before the people of Israel. I will show him how much he must suffer for my name"' (Acts 9:15, 16).

Paul revealed another facet of his call when defending himself before Agrippa: 'I heard a voice saying to me... "Get up and stand on your feet. I have appeared to you to appoint you as a servant and as a witness of what you have seen of me and what I will show you. I will rescue you from your own people and from the Gentiles. I am sending you to open their eyes and turn them from darkness to light, and from the power of Satan to God"' (Acts 26:14–18).

So from the earliest days of his Christian life, Paul not only knew that he was a chosen medium through whom

God would communicate His revelation, but he had a
general idea of what God had planned for his future:
(a) His ministry would take him far from his home; (b) He
would have a special ministry to the Gentiles; (c) It would
involve him in great suffering. Only gradually did he come
to realize that this call was not so much a new purpose of
God for his life, as the culmination of the preparatory
process that began before his birth.

So it is today. The call of the Christian leader is not so
much a new purpose for his life as the discovery of the
purpose for which God brought him into the world. The
Lord had said to his disciples that positions of leadership in
His Kingdom were in the sovereign appointment of His
Father. 'These places belong to those for whom they have
been prepared' (Mk 10:40). Paul recognized this, but he
came only gradually into a clear understanding of what
God's work for him was.

It was only after the Jews had consistently rejected his
message that Paul devoted himself almost exclusively to the
Gentiles. His experience in Corinth brought things to a
head. 'Paul devoted himself exclusively to preaching, testifying to the Jews that Jesus was the Christ. But when the
Jews opposed Paul and became abusive, he shook out his
clothes in protest and said to them, "Your blood be on your
own heads! I am clear of my responsibility. From now on
I will go to the Gentiles"' (Acts 18:5, 6).

Several years after his conversion, this initial call was
renewed and confirmed by the church at Antioch where he
had ministered for a year. 'While they (the leaders) were
worshipping the Lord and fasting, the Holy Spirit said, "Set
apart for me Barnabas and Saul for the work to which I
have called them"' (Acts 13:2). Thus the general call now
became specific, and they joyously set out, 'sent on their
way by the Holy Spirit'.

The first major step in the fulfilment of the Lord's great
commission and the beginning of the grand world-wide

missionary enterprise had been safely negotiated.

Ambition

A leader is usually an ambitious person. Even in his unregenerate days the Apostle had been fiercely ambitious, and conversion did not quench that flame. He could not do things by halves, for there appeared to be an inner compulsion that drove him relentlessly forward. Impatient of the *status quo*, his gaze was always trained on greater achievements and distant horizons.

His unregenerate ambition had focused on effacing the name of the impostor Jesus, exterminating His followers and quenching the growing influence of His church. His burning zeal for Judaism, which he considered the only true religion, drove him to wild excesses: 'Saul was still breathing out murderous threats against the Lord's disciples', the record runs (Acts 9:1).

On several occasions he gave an insight into the state of his heart at this stage: 'I persecuted the followers of this Way to their death, arresting both men and women and throwing them into prison' (Acts 22:4). 'Many a time I went from one synagogue to another to have them punished, and I tried to force them to blaspheme. In my obsession against them, I even went to foreign cities to persecute them' (Acts 26:11). 'I was advancing in Judaism beyond many Jews of my own age and was extremely zealous for the traditions of my fathers' (Gal 1:14).

The loving providence of God is further seen in the manner in which this natural ambition was redirected into spiritually productive channels diametrically opposed to that of former days. His new ambition found a fresh centre in the glory of Christ and the advancement of His kingdom. He nailed his old ambition to the cross and now longed to bring blessing to those whose extermination he had once plotted. 'I long to see you,' he wrote to the believers in

Rome, 'so that I may impart to you some spiritual gift to make you strong' (Rom 1:11).

On two occasions he defines his ambition. The first was to win the approval of the Lord: 'So we make it our goal to please him' (2 Cor 5:9). The approval of Christ was his sufficient reward for any service or suffering. This ambition goaded him along the path of faithful though sacrificial service.

The second related to his career: 'It has always been my ambition to preach the gospel where Christ was not known, so that I would not be building on someone else's foundation' (Rom 15:20). It has been said that he suffered from acute spiritual claustrophobia—the fear of being confined in an enclosed space. He was in the grip of an insatiable passion for advance. He would not be fenced in. Had he not been called to go 'far hence to the Gentiles?' He made it a point of honour to be true to his commission.

He was haunted by the regions beyond. His vision knew no horizons: Corinth, Rome, Spain.

Here as everywhere he was a pattern leader for the Church in coming ages. His missionary zeal fired Henry Martyn who said that he desired 'not to burn out for avarice, to burn out for ambition, to burn out for self, but looking up at that whole burnt-offering, to burn out for God and His work'. A similar ambition has fired the imagination and heart of every great missionary. Like Paul, we too should be ambitious to occupy every unoccupied field or territory for Christ.

It hardly needs to be emphasized that Paul's ambition was essentially selfless and Christ-centred. He was himself the best illustration of the disinterested love which he advocated. He longed to be useful to God and his fellow men and to discharge his debt to both. 'Our hope is that ...our area of activity among you will greatly expand, so that we can preach the gospel in the regions beyond you. For we do not want to boast about work already done in another man's territory (2 Cor 10:15,16).

Motivation

Only powerful motivation could inspire and maintain such a consuming ambition. In a number of incidental statements in his letters, the Apostle revealed some of the motives that inspired his prodigious labours and made him the inspired and inspiring leader he became.

The first in point of time and in order of importance was his unshakable conviction that *Christ was the promised Messiah*, and therefore had the right to the absolute Lordship of his life. The two questions he asked immediately he had seen the heavenly vision, 'Who are you, Lord?' and 'What shall I do, Lord?' centred on these two facts (Acts 9:5; 22:10).

Next to this motive was the compulsive power of *the love of Christ*. 'For Christ's love compels us'—constrains, controls, leaves us no option (2 Cor 5:14). The love that had broken and captured his rebellious heart on the Damascus highway held him in willing vassalage until he met Him in glory. It was this that nerved him for the incredible trials and sufferings and privations that were his lot. This love for Christ inevitably found expression in ardent love of those for whom Christ died.

Paul laboured under an inescapable *sense of obligation*. 'I feel myself under a sort of universal obligation', he wrote. 'I owe something to all men, from cultured Greek to ignorant savage' (Rom 1:14 Phillips). He had the authentic Christian passion to share a great discovery, and this all-embracing obligation leapt over all racial barriers, rode over all cultural differences. He felt himself equally indebted to *all men*, since all were included in the scope of Christ's love and sacrifice. Social status, wealth, poverty, illiteracy alike were all irrelevant. At all costs he must discharge his debt.

Only like souls I see the folk thereunder,
   Bound who should be conquerors,
   Slaves who should be kings.
Hearing their one hope with an empty wonder,
   Sadly contented with a show of things.
Then with a rush the intolerable craving
   Shivers throughout me like a trumpet call,
Oh, to save these, to perish for their saving,
   Die for their life, be offered for them all.

F. W. H. Myers

The fear of the Lord was to him a solemn reality and constituted a powerful motive to seek the lost. 'Since, then, we know what it is to fear the Lord, we try to persuade men' (2 Cor 5:11). He believed there was and is such a thing as the wrath of the God of love. 'The wrath of God is being revealed from heaven against all the godlessness and wickedness of men...' (Rom 1:18). But whenever he referred to the wrath and judgement of God, it was always in tones of the Saviour's mercy; for example, 'The wages of sin is death, but the gift of God is eternal life in Christ Jesus our Lord' (Rom 6:23).

The hope of the return of Christ was to Paul a source of strong motivation. He was deeply influenced by the powers of the world to come. 'Our citizenship is in heaven. And we eagerly await a Saviour from there, the Lord Jesus Christ' (Phil 3:20). This glorious prospect was to him a spur to soul-winning endeavour. 'What is our hope, our joy, or the crown in which we will glory in the presence of our Lord Jesus Christ when he comes? Is it not you? Indeed, you are our glory and joy' (1 Thess 2:19).

Post-graduate courses

F. B. Meyer wrote: 'We all need to go to Arabia to learn lessons like these. The Lord Himself was led up into wilderness. And in one form or another, every soul who has done a great work in the world has passed through similar periods of obscurity, suffering, disappointment or solitude.'[11]

Although the Apostle had enjoyed the advantage of a superb religious and academic training, before he could attain maximum usefulness in achieving God's eternal purpose for the Gentiles, he had to undertake a postgraduate course. His fiery spirit had to be tempered, and yet without any quenching of its zeal.

To achieve this, a period of withdrawal and solitude was necessary, for solitude is an important element in the maturing process. Spiritual leadership does not develop best in the glare of publicity. Further, since God aims at quality in His chosen instruments, time is no object with Him. We are always in a hurry, but He is not.

Unlike many today, he did not rush immediately into his new work, but wisely sought solitude. He desired to be alone to meditate and to relate the present to the past. 'I did not consult any man, nor did I go up to Jerusalem to see those who were apostles before I was, but I went immediately into Arabia and later returned to Damascus' (Gal 1:16,17). Strangely, there is no mention in Luke's record of his stay in Arabia.

Today there is an unhealthy tendency to push young converts into prominence before they have really found their feet. Paul avoided this snare. Probably twelve years of quiet training and evangelistic endeavour elapsed before he launched upon his flaming missionary career.

The exact location of his years of retreat is not certain. Some have thought he went to Sinai, a reasonable conjecture, but Sir William Ramsay's view is that he went to the adjacent country on the east of Damascus.

The revolution in his life had been so devastating that he needed time to adjust his thinking. There, schooled by the Spirit, with infinite leisureliness God taught and trained the chosen messenger who was to open the world to the gospel.

He had to review the whole course of Old Testament truth in the light of the new revelation that had come to him.

The far-reaching, undreamed of implications of the sufferings and death of the Messiah had to be thought through. He now had to formulate his theology along radically different lines. Through these formative days and years, under the Spirit's tuition, he was unconsciously storing his mind with facts and arguments that were to stand him in good stead in the coming days of controversy and opposition. There, too, he dropped the intolerable burden of Pharisaic law-keeping and embraced the doctrine of free, but costly grace.

Following his period of seclusion in Arabia, Paul returned to Damascus (Gal 1:17), and three years later went back to the Holy City. He desired firstly, through fellowship with Peter, to learn more at first hand about the Lord; and secondly, to endeavour to win the rabbis to the new movement. In this he was bitterly disappointed.

'I fell into a trance,' he recounted to the crowds in Jerusalem, 'and saw the Lord speaking: "Quick!" he said to me. "Leave Jerusalem immediately, because they will not accept your testimony about me..." The crowd listened to Paul until he said this. Then they raised their voices and shouted, "Rid the earth of him! He's not fit to live"' (Acts 22:17,18,22).

After a period of ministry in Damascus (Acts 19:9–25), Paul returned to Tarsus where he remained for about eight years. How he filled them is not clear, but we can be sure he was actively propagating his new-found faith. These years of preparatory evangelism culminated in a year of rich experience in the church at Antioch under the guidance of Barnabas. From this church as centre, Paul embarked to fulfil his life charter as apostle to the Gentile world. Important years they were, during which there was a great maturing and deepening of character.

It should be noted by aspiring leaders that Paul proved

himself and approved himself to his own home church and city before moving out into wider spheres of service.

The result of these years of obscurity was that 'when he came forth to his work, he had a message—unborrowed, original, fresh from God'.

3

Paul's Leadership Qualities

'A man is not only what he owes to his parents, friends and teachers, but a man is also what God has made him by calling him to some particular ministry and by endowing him with appropriate natural and spiritual gifts.'[12]

Wherever he went, Paul stood out as a man of unusual authority and force of personality—a man who was every inch a leader. At a gathering of missionary leaders in Shanghai many years ago, D. E. Hoste, who succeeded Hudson Taylor as General Director of the China Inland Mission, was asked his opinion as to what was the mark of a good leader. With his usual whimsical humour he replied, 'If I wanted to discover whether I was a leader, I would look behind me to see who was following!' Paul never lacked followers.

His qualities of character irresistibly lifted him above his colleagues and associates. For example, when he and Barnabas set out on their first missionary journey, the order was 'Barnabas and Saul'. But before long by sheer force of character he outstripped the older man, and we read of 'Saul and Barnabas'. To his credit, it appears that large-hearted Barnabas did not resent the leadership of his younger colleague.

The incident at Lystra where Paul and Barnabas were mistaken for the gods Jupiter and Mercury provides an interesting sidelight (Acts 14:11–20).

There was a myth that these two gods visited Baucis and Philemon in that very area, and rewarded them for their hospitality by turning their humble hut into a palace. They pictured Jupiter as a tall, majestic figure, while Mercury was his messenger and spokesman. The people concluded that the tall, paternal Barnabas was Jupiter and the insignificant Paul was Mercury.

Their conclusion reveals the difference between the oriental and the occidental outlook. We would naturally envisage the leader as the dynamic, energetic person. But in the east they would more likely view as leader the one who sat and allowed his subordinates to do the work. The names allocated to each of the men reflected this concept. At the same time their assessment was an impressive tribute to the authority and persuasiveness of Paul's speech. Despite his 'weakness and fear and much trembling', his words were accompanied by divine power.

How fickle the crowd is! Worshipped as a god one day, and stoned the next! 'The gods have come down to us in human form' (v.11). 'They stoned Paul and dragged him outside the city' (v.19).

In the shipwreck on the way to Rome, when it seemed inevitable that all would be lost, it was Paul who stood out as the heroic figure (Acts 27:27–44). The prisoner commanded the captain; such was his massive personality and moral authority, that the whole crew obeyed his orders without question.

When he stood on trial for his life before Agrippa, it was the prisoner who sentenced the judge rather than the judge who sentenced the prisoner.

He did not exercise his authority in a harsh or arbitrary manner, but neither did he always suffer fools gladly. He was reasonable, and not overbearing. He expressed his own attitude to authority when he wrote to the Corinthians: 'This is why I write these things when I am absent, that when I come I may not have to be harsh in my use of authority—the authority the Lord gave me for building you up, not for tearing you down' (2 Cor 13:10).

Paul's leadership was not perfect, but it provides us with a tremendously encouraging and inspiring example of what it means to continue pressing towards maturity.

His conception of the leader's role in Christian work is reflected in the Greek words he uses in that connection. He is a *steward* (1 Cor 4:2), a word meaning the manager of the household's resources. He is an *administrator* (1 Cor 12:28), a word signifying the helmsman who steers the ship, and thus one who directs the task. He is an *overseer* (Acts 20:28), a word meaning guardian or protector. He is an *elder* (Acts 20:17), implying maturity of Christian experience. He is a *ruler* (Rom 12:8), a word meaning one who stands before the people and leads them. Of course not every leader fills all these roles, but Paul's use of these descriptive words gives some indication of the complexity of the task, and the need for flexibility and adaptability in exercising it.

. The versatility that characterized his own leadership is demonstrated in the variety of tactics he employed in dealing with the problems of differing people and churches.

Sometimes he was kindly and paternal: 'We were gentle among you, like a mother caring for her little children' (1 Thess 2:7,8,11), but when necessity demanded, he thundered: 'I already gave you a warning when I was with you the second time. I now repeat it while absent: On my return I will not spare those who sinned earlier or any of the others' (2 Cor 13:2,3).

Now he was brotherly: 'But, brothers, when we were torn away from you for a short time...out of our intense longing we made every effort to see you, for we wanted to come to you' (1 Thess 2:17,18). Sometimes he uses stinging sarcasm in the hope of bringing them to a better state of mind: 'Already you have all you want! Already you have become rich! You have become kings—and that without us!...We are fools for Christ, but you are so wise in Christ! We are weak, but you are strong! You are honoured, we are dishonoured!' (1 Cor 4:8–10).

Again, he is playful: 'Be that as it may, I have not been a burden to you. Yet, crafty fellow that I am, I caught you by trickery!' (2 Cor 12:16). At other times he gives generous praise: 'For you, brothers, became imitators of God's churches in Judea...You suffered from your own countrymen the same things those churches suffered from the Jews' (1 Thess 2:14). He urges one church to emulate the generosity of another: 'I am not commanding you, but I want to test the sincerity of your love by comparing it with the earnestness of others' (2 Cor 8:8).[13]

Although there is no uniformity in Paul's leadership method, the flexible approach he adopted usually proved to be acceptable and successful.

Like his Master, in training men for leadership Paul focused on individuals as well as addressing the crowds. He poured his life into a small number of men with leadership potential. He did not try to exert a cultic control over their minds, nor did he place his reliance on platform personality or elaborate public relations. His ultimate reliance was on the promised cooperation of the Holy Spirit.

His dynamic leadership left its impression on the whole western world. As R. E. O. White says in assessing the reach of Paul's influence, 'Far beyond his own imagining, or the understanding of his contemporaries, Paul engraved his name deeply on the story of mankind as one of the makers of Europe, and indeed of the whole Western world; for the things he wrote and stood for became the unquestioned assumptions of the whole medieval way of life, upon which modern civilisation in the West was built'.[14]

One striking feature of Paul's leadership was that it did not wane with the passing of the years, nor could prison bars restrict its scope. Even when he was 'Paul the aged', he remained the model and leader of a group of dynamic younger men. The affection he kindled in his followers' hearts was mirrored in the tears that flowed when he told them they would see him no more (Acts 20:36–38).

We will now consider some of the major qualities that contributed to his mastery of men.

Considerateness

Leaders with talents and force of character like those of Paul frequently tend to overpower or override others who are less forceful, and to be insensitive towards the rights and convictions of others. Paul was punctilious in his relationships, and handled difficult situations with rare tact and consideration.

The original meaning of the word 'tact' was the sense of touch, and came to mean skill in dealing with persons or sensitive situations. It is defined as 'intuitive perception, especially a quick and fine perception of what is fit and proper and right'. It includes the idea of ability to conduct delicate negotiations and personal matters in a way that recognizes mutual rights, and yet leads to a harmonious solution.

Paul was thoughtful and sensitive to the rights and feelings of others, and studiously avoided getting wires crossed. He took pains to avoid trespassing on another's sphere of authority. The following passage reveals his respect for the work of others:

> We will not boast of authority we do not have... It is not as though we were trying to claim credit for the work someone else has done among you. Instead, we hope that your faith will grow and that, still within the limits set for us, our work among you will be greatly enlarged. After that, we will be able to preach the Good News to other cities that are far beyond you, where no one else is working; then there will be no question about being in someone else's field (2 Cor 10:13–16 TLB).

His sensitivity is seen uniquely in the tactful manner in which he carried on negotiations with Philemon about Onesimus. 'I did not want to do anything without your consent, so that any favour you do will be spontaneous and not forced' (Philem v.14).

Courage

The test of courage in a leader is his ability to face unpleasant or even devastating facts and situations without panic, and his willingness to take firm action when necessary, even if it is unpopular.

Paul's moral courage matched his physical courage, which was of a very high order. He was deterred neither by prospective sufferings nor present danger, when conscious he was in the path of duty. 'And now, compelled by the Spirit, I am going to Jerusalem, not knowing what will happen to me there. I only know that in every city the Holy Spirit warns me that prison and hardships are facing me' (Acts 20:22,23). He would bravely confront the raging mob for his Master's sake. 'Paul wanted to appear before the crowd, but the disciples would not let him. Even some of the officials of the province, friends of Paul, sent him a message begging him not to venture into the theatre' (Acts 19:30,31). He realized that it is not always our duty to avoid danger.

His was not a courage that knew no fear. 'I came to you in weakness and fear, and with much trembling', he told the Corinthians (1 Cor 2:3). A stolid indifference to danger is not a sign of true courage. The man who does not know fear cannot know courage. Paul knew fear, but he also knew that God had not given him 'a spirit of fear,' but a spirit of power (2 Tim 1:7).

He displayed to a remarkable degree that ideal balance of mind, so esteemed by the Greeks, that veers neither to the right nor to the left. His courage did not slip into rashness on the one hand nor timidity on the other. His letters reveal how fearlessly yet tenderly he grasped the nettle of a critical situation, or the writing of a difficult letter, or the administering of deserved rebuke. He was not prepared to allow things to go by default merely to spare himself the heartbreak of an act of deserved discipline. What courage he displayed when, as a comparative newcomer, he rebuked the great Peter for his dissembling. 'When Peter came to Antioch, I opposed him to his face, because he was in the wrong' (Gal 2:11).

Decisiveness

One of the seven essential ingredients of effective military leadership laid down by Field-Marshal Montgomery was the power of clear decision. Paul qualifies here too, for this was a key feature of his character which he displayed at the very time of his conversion.

When the heavens burst open and he saw the exalted Christ, his first question was, 'Who are you, Lord?' The answer, 'I am Jesus of Nazareth whom you are persecuting', toppled his entire theological universe, but he immediately accepted the implications of his discovery. An absolute capitulation to the Son of God was the only possible response, and in his whole-souled way he decided on the spot that it would be unreserved allegiance and obedience. This led to his second question, 'What shall I do, *Lord*?' (Acts 22:8,10).

Vacillation or indecision were foreign to his nature. Once he was sure of the facts, he moved to a swift decision. To be granted light was to follow it. To see his duty was to do it. Once he is sure of the will of God, the effective leader will go into action regardless of consequences. He will be willing to burn his bridges behind him and accept responsibility for failure as well as for success.

Procrastination and vacillation are fatal to leadership. A

sincere though mistaken decision is better than no decision. Indeed, no decision *is* a decision, for it is a decision that the present situation is acceptable. In most decisions the difficulty is not in knowing what we ought to do, but in summoning the moral purpose to come to a decision about it. This was no problem to Paul.

Encouragement

Whether or not it was because of his earlier associations with Barnabas, named by his colleagues Son of Encouragement, Paul himself specialized in this ministry. Encouragement is a constantly recurring note in his letters to churches, especially when they are passing through fiery trials. Though himself so strong in character and in faith, he was not exempt from discouragement or depression. He reached a high plane of triumph in Christian living, but he did not attain it overnight.

'God, who comforts the downcast, comforted us by the coming of Titus,' he testified (2 Cor 7:6). He further claimed: '*I have learned* to be content, whatever the circumstances' (Phil 4:11). The implication is that this had not always been the case, but he had at last mastered the secret of rising above discouraging circumstances. It had been something he had to learn, so we can take courage.

In his second letter to the Corinthians, in which he rejoices that his sterner first letter had achieved its purpose, Paul shares with them some secrets he had learned that enabled him to rise above discouragement.

Twice he uses the phrase 'we do not lose heart', (2 Cor 4:1,16), and from the context we can glean the reason. In chapter 3 he had been describing the radiant glory of the New Covenant of grace, as compared with the Old Covenant of law, and in chapter 3 verse 18 he reveals the secret of sharing and reflecting that radiance.

'We do not lose heart' is a strong statement, and alternative translations highlight this; for example, 'We never give up'; 'we don't get discouraged'; 'we never collapse'. There must be strong motivation to achieve such a desirable end.

One reason why Paul never lost heart was because *he had been entrusted with a glorious ministry*. 'Therefore, since through God's mercy we have this ministry, we do not lose heart' (2 Cor 4:1).

Paul was very conscious that his misguided persecuting zeal had disqualified him for God's service, but he had obtained 'mercy' and 'been entrusted with this commission' (NEB). He was not a self-confident, self-made man. 'Our competence comes from God,' he confessed, 'He has made us competent as ministers of a new covenant' (2 Cor 3:5,6). He never got over the wonder that he had been so trusted by God.

Here was a revolutionary message to proclaim. It is difficult for us to realize how incredible it must have seemed to the Jews, for it was a complete reversal of the Old Covenant on which their whole religious life was based. The inexorable 'thou shalt, thou shalt not' had been replaced by the divine undertaking, 'I will, I will'. The New Covenant came with the assurance of divine enabling (Jer 31:31–34; Ezek 36:25–29; Heb 8:8–13). It was not a message for a spiritual elite, but was tailored especially to meet the need of people who had failed—a message especially for failures!

'When I have such a glorious message', said Paul, 'no wonder I do not lose heart!' It is when we lose the sense of wonder at the message with which we have been entrusted that we lose heart.

He had also *the assurance of being endowed with new divine strength every day*. 'Therefore we do not lose heart. Though outwardly we are wasting away, yet inwardly we are being renewed day by day' (2 Cor 4:16). In the midst of the wear and tear and sufferings to which he was exposed, his body was indeed wasting away, but that was not the whole story. A counter-process was taking place. At the same time his inner being was experiencing spiritual renewal—fresh accessions of strength from God. 'No wonder we don't give up!' Paul exclaims.

Our heavenly Father knows the strains and stresses involved in our service. He is not insensitive to the cost at which we often carry it out. He knows when we near the point of collapse, and to counteract this, He promises daily renewal. Why do we not appropriate more from God when there is such ample provision?

Paul was very susceptible to external influences and felt loneliness acutely, but news of the spiritual progress of individuals or churches greatly cheered and encouraged him. 'Therefore, brothers, in all our distress and persecution, we were encouraged about you because of your faith' (1 Thess 3:7). He found that encouragement was a two-way thing.

Faith and vision

'There was no credibility gap with God as far as Paul was concerned. The faith in God's word which Paul displayed on the high seas was typical of the confidence he had in Him to do everything He promised.'[15]

'I have faith in God that it will happen just as he told me' (Acts 27:25).

It is one of the important functions of a spiritual leader to communicate to those who follow the faith and vision which he himself possesses. Paul was nothing if not a man of faith. His trust in Christ was absolute, and wherever he went he left behind him people whose faith had been quickened and renewed.

In his letters he had many things to say about faith that reveal his own insights. He saw faith as the principle of the Christian's daily life. 'We live by faith, not by sight' (2 Cor 5:7). A craving for outward signs or miracles, or for inward feelings to bolster faith, he regarded as a sign of spiritual immaturity. Faith is occupied with the invisible and spiritual. Sight is concerned with the tangible and visible. Sight concedes reality only to things present and seen. 'Faith forms a solid ground for what is hoped for, a conviction of unseen realities' (Heb 11:1 Berkeley).

Faith is confidence, reliance, trust, and has its dealings directly with God. Indeed, 'without faith it is impossible to please God' (Heb 11:6). Paul's faith in God was a childlike, effortless trust that was never betrayed. With such a God as Scripture revealed, he was as much at home in the realm of the impossible as of the possible. His God knew no limitations, and therefore was worthy of limitless trust.

It was Paul who told us that 'faith comes from hearing the message, and the message is heard through the word of Christ' (Rom 10:17). It does not come through introspection but by being occupied with what God has said. If we desire to have faith, we must first discover a divinely authenticated fact on which it can rest. Paul reminds us that this was the secret of the father of the faithful, Abraham: 'He did not waver through unbelief regarding the promise of God, but was strengthened in his faith and gave glory to God' (Rom 4:20). Faith feeds on the pledged word of God.

Faith is vision. Paul was able to see things that were invisible to many of his more earthbound colleagues. Elisha's servant saw with great vividness the vastness of the encircling army. Elisha's faith enabled him to see the invincible and environing hosts of heaven. His faith imparted vision.

Where others saw difficulties, Paul saw new opportunities. 'I will stay on at Ephesus until Pentecost, because a great door for effective work has opened to me, and there are many who oppose me' (1 Cor 16:8,9). So far from deterring him, the great opposition acted only as a stimulus to enter the open door.

Although essentially a realist, Paul was none the less an

optimist. No pessimist ever made an inspiring leader. The man who sees the difficulties so clearly that he does not discern the possibilities will never inspire others.

Friendship

'You can tell a man by his friends.' There is more than a grain of truth in this adage. A man's ability to make and maintain enduring friendships will in general be the measure of his ability to lead.

Unlike many other great leaders Paul's was not the 'greatness of isolation'. He was essentially gregarious, and possessed in a unique degree the power of capturing and holding the intense love and loyalty of the friends with whom he freely mixed. His love for them was genuine and ran deep.

You seldom find him working alone. He became desperately lonely when isolated. 'He had a genius for friendship', wrote Harrington C. Lees. 'No man in the New Testament made fiercer enemies, but few men in the world have had better friends. They cluster around him so thickly that we are apt to lose their personality in their devotion.'[16]

His happiness was always heightened by the presence of his friends, and he did his best work when accompanied by trusted fellow-workers.

Inevitably Paul often involved his friends in all sorts of risks for Christ's sake, but they followed him cheerfully, because they were assured of his love and concern for them. His letters glow with the warmth of his affection and appreciation of his fellow-workers.

It was John R. Mott's counsel to 'rule by the heart. When argument and logic and other forms of persuasion fail, fall back on the heart—genuine friendship'. Personal friendliness will do more to draw the best out of other people than prolonged and even successful argument. Paul was a master of this art.

P.T.L.–C

'Nothing can take the place of affection', wrote A. W. Tozer in his biography of R. A. Jaffray. 'Those who have it in generous measure have a magic power over men.'

> Hearts I have won, of sister or of brother,
>   Quick on earth, or buried in the sod,
> Lo, every heart awaiteth me, another
>   Friend in the blameless family of God.
>
>   *F. W. H. Myers*

One great secret of Paul's friendships was his capacity to love unselfishly, even if his love was met with no return. 'So I will very gladly spend for you everything I have and expend myself as well. If I love you more, will you love me less?' (2 Cor 12:15).

Paul's friendship with Luke, the beloved physician, is an example of intimacy between men of similar age and tastes. His friendship with Barnabas was also very warm and, happily, outlived his acute difference over the defection of John Mark. His relationship with Timothy is a model of friendship between an older and a younger man. Many women, too, were numbered among the friends whom he remembered with affection (Rom 16).

His capacity for friendship was a prime factor in his ability to inspire others to similar qualities of leadership.

Modest self-appraisal

In his preaching and writing, Paul unselfconsciously uses his own experiences as illustrations, and shares his own inner battles, frustrations and failures. He does not denigrate his own sincerity and integrity (2 Cor 1:23; Rom 9:1,2), but neither does he exalt himself unduly. 'For by the grace given me I say to every one of you: Do not think of yourself more highly than you ought, but rather think of yourself with sober judgment, in accordance with the measure of faith God has given you' (Rom 12:3).

He was fully conscious of his own failures and shortcomings, since his standard was a maturity measured by 'the whole measure of the fulness of Christ' (Eph 4:13). He confessed to the limitation of his own attainment: 'Not that I have already obtained all this, or have already been made perfect, but I press on to take hold on that for which Christ Jesus took hold on me' (Phil 3:12). Instead of discouraging him from further moral endeavour, his recognition of his own shortcomings only caused him to 'strain towards that which is ahead'.

His incidental sayings reflect his self-image.

> What is Paul? Only a servant, through whom you came to believe (1 Cor 3:5).

> I came to you in weakness and fear, and with much trembling (1 Cor 2:3).

> When I preach the gospel, I cannot boast, for I am compelled to preach . . . I am simply discharging the trust committed to me (1 Cor 9:16,17).

> Not that we are competent to claim anything for ourselves, but our competence comes from God (2 Cor 3:5).

And yet, with all this very modest (though not morbid) self-appraisal, Paul daringly exhorts the Corinthians: 'Therefore I urge you to imitate me' (1 Cor 4:16). But later in the same epistle he adds an important rider: 'Follow my example, *as I follow the example of Christ*' (1 Cor 11:1). Holding up his life as an example was not a sign of pride, for what he was and what he had achieved had been done by Christ. 'I will not venture to speak of anything except what Christ accomplished through me' (Rom 15:18).

> Aye, for this Paul, a scorn and a despising,
>
> Weak as you know him and the wretch you see,—

Even in these eyes shall ye behold Him rising,
   Strength in infirmities and Christ in me.

F. W. H. Myers

Paul knew his own worth and would not allow his denigrators to underestimate him. 'I may not be a trained speaker, but I do have knowledge. We have made this perfectly clear to you in every way' (2 Cor 11:6).

Sometimes, although it was distasteful to him, he felt compelled to 'boast' in defence of his apostolic office, but he usually accompanied it with an apology. 'If I must boast, I will boast of the things that show my weaknesses...Even if I should choose to boast, I would not be a fool, because I would be speaking the truth' (2 Cor 11:30; 12:5,6). It was only with reluctance that he spoke of his sufferings (2 Cor 11:23–33).

This delicate and wholesome balance between undue self-depreciation and self-exaltation affords a wonderful model for the Christian leader.

Paul was generous in his appraisal of others, and was totally free of envy of the success or gifts of another. He delighted to associate fellow-workers with himself, even young ones, on terms of equality. 'We are God's fellow-workers' (1 Cor 3:9). Speaking of Timothy he wrote: 'If Timothy comes, see to it that he has nothing to fear while he is with you, for he is carrying on the work of the Lord, just as I am' (1 Cor 16:10). He referred to Titus as his partner (2 Cor 8:23). It is small wonder that these younger men to whom he freely delegated responsibility would have done anything for him.

Humility

Humility is not included in the prospectus of the world's leadership courses, where prominence, publicity and self-advertisement loom large. Speaking to the disciples, Jesus said, 'Whoever wants to become great among you must be your servant' (Mk 10:43). Paul followed closely in the steps of his Lord in this respect. 'Paul had none of the self-will, the exclusive assertiveness of the consciously great man.'[17]

He lived in the humility of a great repentance. While he did not morbidly dwell on it, he never forgot that he had ruthlessly persecuted the church of God; and when his enemies said he was not fit to live, he did not dispute their assessment. An ever-present sense of indebtedness caused him to have a humble estimate of himself. He had no desire to have a reputation higher than he had earned. 'Even if I should choose to boast, I would not be a fool, because I would be speaking the truth. But I refrain, so no one will think more of me than is warranted by what I do or say' (2 Cor 12:6).

He warned the Colossian Christians to beware of a self-conscious, ascetic humility, which is really the subtlest form of pride. 'Do not let anyone who delights in false humility and the worship of angels disqualify you for the prize...He has lost connection with the head...' (Col 2:18,19).

Paul's humility was a progressive quality, deepening with the passing years.

For I am the least of the apostles and do not even deserve to be called an apostle (1 Cor 15:9).

Although I am less than the least of all God's people, this grace was given me: to preach to the Gentiles the unsearchable riches of Christ (Eph 3:8).

Christ Jesus came into the world to save sinners—of whom I am the worst (1 Tim 1:15).

While he was genuinely humble and without mock-modesty, Paul was not at all backward when it came to defending his apostolic office and authority. 'I am afraid... your minds may somehow be led astray from your sincere and pure devotion to Christ. For if someone comes to you and preaches a Jesus other than the Jesus we preached... you put up with it easily enough. But I do not think I am in the least inferior to those "super-apostles"' (2 Cor 11:4,5). One constantly marvels at the sane balance he observes in sensitive areas.

Letter-writing

In any leadership position, the ability to communicate clearly and effectively, whether in correspondence or in other literary work, is a quality much to be desired. Where it is lacking, misunderstandings very quickly arise. Paul, as in so much else, was a master of this art. Whether his letters were written in the midst of a busy itinerant ministry or from the unwelcome solitude of his prison cell, he succeeded in injecting his personality very vividly into his writing.

It is in our unstudied correspondence that we reveal our true selves, and in his letters the real Paul peeps out on every page. We know more of the man from his letters than from any other historical source. They are models for any Christian leader, combining as they do clarity of thought and felicity of expression. They reveal keen spiritual insight coupled with sound commonsense and loving concern.

The rich profusion of thought and the excitement of the truth he wished to convey sometimes caused him to break his train of thought, or leave sentences unfinished. In the early days of the Church Irenaeus defended Paul, because he 'frequently uses a transposed order in his sentences, due to the rapidity of his discourses, and the impetus of the Spirit who is in him'.

Not all his letters were pleasant and easy to write. Indeed, in his second letter to the Corinthians, he referred to his previous letter which contained exhortation and rebuke in these words: 'For I wrote to you out of great distress and anguish of heart and with many tears, not to grieve you but to let you know the depth of my love for you' (2 Cor 2:4).

When he had a difficult letter to write, he was careful to dip his pen in tears and not in acid.

After he had written his strong letter to the erring Corinthians, his tender pastor's heart caused him to wonder whether he had been too severe. He could not rest for anxiety lest they should misunderstand what he had written. 'Even if I caused you sorrow by my letter', he wrote afterwards, 'I do not regret it. Though I did regret it—I see that my letter hurt you, but only for a little while—yet now I am happy, not because you were made sorry, but because your sorrow led you to repentance. For you became sorrowful as God intended and so were not harmed in any way by us' (2 Cor 7:8,9).

In writing a letter of this nature, Paul's objective was not to win an argument, but to resolve a spiritual problem, restore harmony and unity and produce a growing maturity.

From Paul we learn that, while it is important to couch our letters in clear speech so that the meaning is plain, it is even more important that they breathe a spirit of loving concern. Letters are an unsatisfactory medium of communication. They cannot smile, they have no eyes to express love when they are saying something difficult. We should therefore take extra care to see that they are warm in tone. When a much-blessed friend of the author wrote a letter that could cause hurt feelings, he made a practice of holding it over-night and reading it again in the morning, to make sure that its spirit was right.

Encouragement and inspiration abounded in Paul's correspondence. He always aimed at the spiritual enrichment of the recipients, but that did not mean that he refrained from faithful correction and rebuke where that was called for. 'Have I now become your enemy by telling you the truth?' he asked the Galatian believers... 'My dear children, for whom I am again in the pains of childbirth until Christ is formed in you, how I wish I could be with you now and change my tone, because I am perplexed about you' (Gal 4:16,19,20).

Letters were an important part of Paul's follow-up programme, and contributed greatly to the growth and development of the churches to which he wrote. George Whitefield, the silver-tongued evangelist, emulated Paul in this area. It was said that after preaching to large crowds, he would often sit up until 3 a.m. writing letters of instruction and encouragement to new converts.

No one would have been more surprised than Paul had anyone told him that his pastoral letters would become one of the most influential forces in the religious and intellectual history of the world. They were written as part of his ordinary day's work, and with 'no thought of fame or futurity'. While they were not formal treatises and at times lacked literary polish, they have an eloquence and appeal of their own. Their influence through the ages cannot be estimated.

Tolstoy adds another thought: 'How strange and odd it would have seemed to the educated Romans of the middle of the first century that the letters addressed by a wandering Jew to his friends and pupils would have a hundred, a thousand, a hundred thousand times more readers and more circulation than all the poems, odes and elegies and elegant epistles of the authors of those days—and yet this is what has happened'.

Listening

An aspiring politician approached Oliver Wendell Holmes and asked him how to get elected to office. He replied: 'To be able to listen to others in a sympathetic and under-standing manner is, perhaps, the most effective mechanism in the world for getting along with people, and tying up their friendship for good. Too few people practise the "white magic" of being good listeners'.

A missionary once spoke to the author about his senior. 'He doesn't listen to me', he complained. 'Before I have a chance to really state the problem, he is giving the answer.' This is the failing of the compulsive talker. He is afraid of a moment's silence. But the art of listening to one's colleagues must be mastered if the leader is to get at the root of the problems to be solved. Otherwise he will be likely to deal only with the symptom while the dire malady remains untreated.

When he was canvassing for votes at the time Singapore was moving towards independence, Lee Kuan Yew, who became Prime Minister of the Republic, spent every Saturday afternoon and evening in a different one of the fifty-one electoral precincts. He invited any citizen with problems to meet him and tell him their problem. He listened to their woes and wherever possible endeavoured to secure redress. And the result? He was re-elected in every one of the precincts. He believed in and practised the therapy of listening, and reaped the reward. A sympathetic ear is an invaluable asset.

Listening is a genuine endeavour to understand what the other person desires to unload, and to do it without prejudging the issue. A problem is often half-answered when it is brought out into the open and shared with a sympathetic listener. One missionary who became a casualty moaned, 'If only he had listened to me! I needed someone with whom to share my problem.'

Sensitivity to the needs of others is better expressed by listening than by talking. Leaders too frequently convey the impression, unconsciously and certainly unintentionally, that they are too busy to listen. Both they and the colleague are the losers. Happy is the leader who, in the midst of pressing duties, gives the impression that there is ample time to share the problem. He is the one who is most likely to provide a solution. Time spent listening is not time wasted.

Writing of Napoleon, D. E. Hoste said, 'He was a good listener and possessed in a high degree the gift of applying the special knowledge of others to a particular set of circumstances. Doesn't history show that every truly great man is more or less made on these lines?'[18]

Reading between the lines, it is not difficult to sense that Paul was a man who knew the value of listening. When the church in Corinth was floundering amid a welter of problems for which they had no solution, they knew they would find an understanding heart and a listening ear in Paul. His first letter was his answer to their enquiries.

Magnanimity

The transforming miracle of conversion is seldom more strikingly illustrated than in the case of Paul. The man who rushed down the Damascus road on his gruesome mission was a fanatical bigot with a closed mind. The blinded man who was led back to Damascus had within him the making of a generous and broadminded saint. The narrow-minded Pharisee would go to any length to destroy the church. The broadminded Christian would now go to any length to defend it and extend it.

What brought about the change? It was not only that he had seen the living Christ, but that Christ now dwelt in his heart and had immeasurably enlarged it and widened its horizons. The Spirit of God had poured the boundless love of God into his heart (Rom 5:5), and the bigot now became tolerant.

When some of his implacable opponents were 'preaching Christ out of envy and rivalry...supposing they can stir up trouble', it would have been very easy for the Paul of old to have hurled blistering denunciations at them. The new Paul says, 'But what does it matter? The important thing is that in every way, whether from false motives or true, Christ is preached. And because of this I rejoice' (Phil 1:15–18).

But it should be said that he was not so tolerant as to compromise the essential truths of the faith, nor was he so broad as to be shallow.

Patience

Was John Chrysostom wrong in his judgement when he called patience the Queen of Virtues? Our usage of the word is too negative and passive to convey the rich meaning of the word Paul used so frequently. In his writings William Barclay has invested the word with a very full and attractive significance. Commenting on the word as used in 2 Peter 1:5,6 (KJV): 'Add to your faith virtue; and to virtue knowledge; and to knowledge temperance; and to temperance *patience*', he writes: 'The word never means the spirit that sits with folded hands and simply bears things. It is victorious endurance, masculine constancy under trial. It is Christian steadfastness, the brave and courageous acceptance of everything life can do to us, and the transmuting of even the worst into another step on the upward way. It is the courageous and triumphant ability to bear things; which enables a man to pass breaking point and not break, and always to greet the unseen with a cheer.'[19]

Professor Barclay could have been drawing a word picture of the apostle, so fully does Paul illustrate the quality he is commending.

This quality or virtue is essential, especially in relationships with people. It is here that most of us break down. Paul lost out at this point in his disagreement with Barnabas, and when he spoke disrespectfully to the high priest. But these were rare exceptions and not the rule.

The man who is impatient with the weakness and failings of others will be defective in leadership. 'We who are strong ought to bear with the failings of the weak' (Rom 15:1). The good leader knows how to adapt his pace to that of his slower brother.

Patience is especially essential when we seek to lead by persuasion rather than by command. It is not always easy to bring another to see one's viewpoint and act accordingly, but there is great value in cultivating the art of persuasion that allows the individual to make his own decision.

> Our life is like the dial of a clock,
> The hands are God's hands passing o'er and o'er,
> The short hand is the hand of Discipline
> The long, the Hand of Mercy evermore.

> Slowly and surely discipline must pass,
> And God speaks at each stroke His Word of Grace,
> But ever on the hand of mercy moves,
> With blessing sixty-fold the trials efface.

> Each moment counts a blessing from our God,
> Each hour a lesson in the school of love,
> Both hands are fastened to a pivot sure,
> The great unchanging heart of God above.

> *S. M. Zwemer*

Self-discipline

A leader is able to lead others because he disciplines himself. He who does not know how to bow to discipline imposed from without, who does not know how to obey, will not make a good leader. Nor will the one who has not learned to impose discipline within his own life. Those who scorn scriptural or legal authority, or rebel against it, rarely qualify for high leadership positions.

Paul imposed on himself a rigorous inner discipline in two areas:

He waged war with his body. 'I do not run like a man running aimlessly; I do not fight like a man beating the air. No, I beat my body and make it my slave so that after I have preached to others, I myself will not be disqualified for the prize' (1 Cor 9:26,27).

He was expressing a genuine fear, a real possibility. He had not yet completed the course, even his vast experience and great successes did not render him immune to the subtle temptations of the body. In order that his ministry should not be short-circuited, he was willing to bring his bodily appetites under as strict self-discipline as did the athletes in the arena.

> Well let me sin, but not with my consenting,
> Well let me die, but willing to be whole:
> Never, O Christ—so stay me from relenting—
> Shall there be truce betwixt my flesh and soul.

> *F. W. H. Myers*

The Christian leader is open to the danger of being defeated through over-indulgence of physical appetites or through laziness, and this calls for stern self-discipline. At the other end of the scale is an excess of physical activity which can lead to fatigue and exhaustion. The leader must be prepared to work harder than his colleagues, but an exhausted man easily falls prey to the adversary. We should be alert to guard against both extremes.

He waged war with his thoughts. 'The weapons we fight with are not the weapons of the world. On the contrary, they have divine power to demolish strongholds. We demolish arguments and every pretension that sets itself up against the knowledge of God, and we take captive every thought to make it obedient to Christ' (2 Cor 10:4,5).

Paul knew that sin has its genesis in the thought life, so he made it his constant endeavour to prevent his thoughts from wandering and to bring them under the control of Christ.

More than strong willpower is needed to bring and keep

both body and mind under divine control, but God has made provision for this. 'The fruit of the Spirit is *self-control*' (Gal 5:23). Paul's secret was that he was 'full of the Spirit', and this desirable fruit was produced in his life in abundance.

Sincerity and integrity

In his letters, Paul lays himself bare to a degree few would be willing to do, and in so doing leaves the impression of a man who is utterly sincere. During World War II, the young Billy Graham was invited by Sir Winston Churchill to meet him in the Parliament Buildings in London. When he was ushered into the room, to his dismay he found himself in the presence of the whole British Cabinet. Churchill soon put him at his ease, and Billy had the opportunity of sharing his faith. After he had left the room, Churchill remarked to his colleagues, 'There goes a sincere man'. Sincerity is an unconscious quality that is self-revealing.

Even before his conversion Paul showed this quality. 'I thank God, whom I serve, as my forefathers did, with a clear conscience' (2 Tim 1:3). Throughout his life he was ingenuously conscious of his own integrity, and he worked at maintaining it. 'So I strive always to keep my conscience clear before God and man' (Acts 24:16). He was no more sincere when building up the Church than when he was destroying it. He was desperately wrong, but he did not compromise his conscience, misguided as it was.

He did not shrink from God's scrutiny and could say, 'My conscience is clear', but he hastens to add, 'but that does not make me innocent. It is the Lord who judges me' (1 Cor 4:4). He appealed to God to attest his sincerity. 'Unlike so many, we do not peddle the word of God for profit. On the contrary, in Christ we speak before God with sincerity, like men sent from God' (2 Cor 2:17).

Spiritual wisdom

When men were to be selected for a position of leadership, one of the two qualities specified was 'wisdom'—an essential for good leadership. 'Choose seven men from among you who are known to be full of the Spirit and wisdom' (Acts 6:3). Wisdom is more than knowledge, which is the mere accumulation of facts. It is more than intellectual acumen, it is heavenly insight. Spiritual wisdom involves the knowledge of God and of the intricacies of the human heart. It is the right application of knowledge in moral and spiritual matters, in meeting perplexing situations and complex human relationships. It is a quality that restrains a leader from rash or eccentric action, and imparts a necessary balance.

> Knowledge and wisdom, far from being one,
> Have at times no connection. Knowledge dwells
> In heads replete with thoughts of other men:
> Wisdom, in minds attentive to their own.
> Knowledge is proud that he has learned so much,
> Wisdom is humble, that he knows no more.

Anon

The high place that Paul gives to spiritual wisdom is seen in the way he constantly contrasts it with the vaunted wisdom of the world. 'Do not deceive yourselves. If any one of you thinks he is wise by the standards of this age, he should become a "fool" so that he may become wise. For the wisdom of this world is foolishness in God's sight' (1 Cor 3:18,19).

Paul frequently prayed that his converts and churches might grow in wisdom. 'We have not stopped praying for you and asking God to fill you with the knowledge of his will through all spiritual wisdom and understanding' (Col 1:9). It characterized his preaching. 'We proclaim him,

admonishing and teaching everyone with all wisdom, so
that we may present everyone perfect in Christ' (Col 1:28).
Wisdom will characterize the ministry of the Spirit-filled
leader. 'Let the word of Christ dwell in you richly as you
teach and admonish one another with all wisdom' (Col
3:16).

It is to Paul we owe the revelation that 'Christ Jesus has
become for us wisdom from God' (1 Cor 1:30).

Zeal and intensity

Like his Master, Paul was wholehearted and zealous in all
his work for God. The family of our Lord, as they observed
His intense zeal, 'went to take charge of him, for they said,
"He is out of his mind"' (Mk 3:21). King Festus said the
same of Paul. 'At this point Festus interrupted Paul's
defence. "You are out of your mind, Paul!" he shouted.
"Your great learning is driving you insane"' (Acts 26:24).
The worldly mind equates zeal for God with insanity, but in
God's sight it is of the highest value.

When he spoke to the crowd at the temple of his unregenerate days, Paul claimed: 'Under Gamaliel I was thoroughly
trained in the law of our fathers and was just as zealous for
God as any of you are today' (Acts 22:3). But his zeal led
him into the terrible excesses which afterwards were his
greatest grief.

Paul carried over into his new life all his old intensity, but
the Spirit directed it into new and vastly productive channels. The word 'zeal' means 'to boil up'—the enthusiasm
that irresistibly bubbles up in the heart.

When the disciples saw their Master in the temple, ablaze
with holy zeal and flaming with sinless anger, they were
astounded at this display of intense zeal, until 'they
remembered that it is written, "Zeal for your house will
consume me"' (Ps 69:9; Jn 2:17).

In this quality Paul sought to emulate his Lord. A perusal

of his letters and discourses reveals that the ideal he entertained for his converts was a mind aflame with the truth of God, a heart ablaze with the love of God, and a will fired with a passion for the glory of God. It was the absence of these qualities that brought our Lord's solemn words to the church at Laodicea (Rev 3:15–16). Such a charge could not be laid at Paul's door. It is the zealous, enthusiastic leader who most deeply and permanently impresses his followers.

Paul incidentally reveals the secret of his unabating zeal in Romans 12:11 which Archbishop H. C. Lees renders: 'Not slothful in business; kept at boiling-point by the Holy Spirit; doing bondservice for the Master'. The Holy Spirit is the central furnace that maintains our intensity and zeal. In all of us there is a subtle tendency to 'cool off', and we constantly need this warming ministry of the Holy Spirit, who kindles the fuel we feed to the fire.

When he entered the Interpreter's house, Bunyan's Christian was perplexed as he observed a man pouring water on the fire, and yet the flames only leapt higher. His mystification was dispelled when he saw at the back of the fire, another man pouring oil on the flames. In a world when there are all too many ready to pour cold water, this is the gracious ministry of the Spirit.

4

Paul's View of God

What comes to our minds when we think
of God is the most important thing about us.

A. W. Tozer[20]

The Apostle's conception of God shaped his theology and
motivated his service. It was fundamental to the nature of
his leadership. As J. B. Phillips demonstrated in his book,
Your God Is Too Small, an inadequate view of God will
limit and adversely affect all we attempt to do.

Paul's faith was built on the doctrine of the Trinity. The
Apostles' Creed would be a summary of the crucial tenets
of his faith which was essentially Trinitarian. 'I believe in
God the Father Almighty...and in Jesus Christ His only
Son our Lord...I believe in the Holy Spirit.' He conceived
of 'God in the sublime majesty of His Being as one God in
three Persons. Within the unity of His Being there is a
distinction of "Persons" whom we call the Father, the Son
and the Holy Spirit.'[21]

To Paul God was the great Reality and he felt no necessity
to argue for His existence. His was a God who was sovereign
in power, but sympathetic towards human frailty and
solicitous for human welfare. Life without God was
inconceivable.

His ideas of God were shaped by the Old Testament

66

records of God's dealings with His people. He had no problem with the supernatural.

One way in which we can discover his conception of God is to study the method by which he sought to strengthen his young protégés, Timothy and Titus, for their demanding service—and here is a valuable lesson in leadership for all. *He aimed to give them a greater God*—to impress them with the greatness and majesty of the God whom they were privileged to serve. His purpose was achieved through the varied titles for God he employed in his pastoral letters, each of which revealed some fresh facet of His greatness and glory.

Consider some of the titles of God that shaped Paul's theology and directed his actions.

God the Father

The blessed God

'The glorious gospel of the blessed God' (1 Tim 1:11). Rotherham translates it, 'the gospel of the glory of *the happy God*'. This rather startling title describes God, not as One who is the object of blessing, but One who Himself enjoys fullness of joy. He lives in the atmosphere of His own eternal joy (Heb 1:9). Jesus had a surplus of joy that He bequeathed to His disciples.

The title 'blessed' is applied to God, for two reasons. First, He is entirely *self-sufficient*. We are constantly striving to become what we are not and to supply what we lack. God needs no one or nothing to complement Him. Secondly, He is *absolute perfection*. The sum total of all virtues is resident in Him. He is the God of all blessedness, in whom nothing is lacking or in excess. So Paul encourages Timothy to believe that the gospel he is to preach arises out of an environment of joy—the happy heart of God.

The King eternal, immortal, invisible, the only God

'Now to the King eternal, immortal, invisible, the only God, be honour and glory for ever and ever' (1 Tim 1:17).

As Paul surveyed God's amazing grace to the chief of sinners in verse 15, he spontaneously burst into a doxology that unveils the nature and attributes of God. It affords unique glimpses of His glory.

(a) '*King of all ages*' (NEB). Man is a creature of time bound by clocks and calendars—God is King of all ages. His power and sovereignty are demonstrated in every age. He is the absolute Ruler of the ages of time. He uses those who try to destroy His church to build it. He overrules evil for good. He moves with immense patience through the ages towards the fulfilment of His eternal purpose. 'He fixed the epochs of their history and the limits of their territory,' Paul declared (Acts 17:26 NEB). He directs the events of each era of world history to its appointed goal. He weaves out of seemingly contradictory events a harmonious and beautiful pattern that reflects His own perfection.

(b) '*Immortal*'. God is incorruptible, imperishable, not subject to the aging process of time and change, decay or death. Immortality is in God by essence, in us only by gift, derived from Him. He never changes. 'I the Lord do not change' (Mal 3:6).

(c) '*Invisible*'. No immediate and full vision of God is possible to man, for He has chosen to remain unseen except in Christ who said, 'He who has seen me has seen the Father' (Jn 14:9)—and even then we see Him only by faith. In Christ we can now see Him who is invisible (Jn 1:18). The finite can never fully comprehend the infinite. Even Moses saw only the afterglow when God had passed by (Ex 33:22,23).

(d) '*The only God*'. There is no other like Him. 'With whom will you compare Me?' (Is 46:5) He asks. He is solitary, yet not aloof or isolated as were the Greek gods—unique in essence and attributes.

The living God (1 Tim 3:15). It was this that distinguished Israel's God from the heathen gods. Paul's church was not a temple of dead idols, but of a living, active, beneficent God. 'What mortal has ever heard the voice of the living God speaking out of fire, as we have, and survived?' (Deut 5:26).

King of kings and Lord of lords

> God, the blessed and only Ruler, the King of kings and Lord of lords, who alone is immortal, and who lives in unapproachable light, whom no one has seen or can see (1 Tim 6:15,16).

How easily Paul bursts into doxology! This is one of the finest doxologies in Scripture, each of the seven titles stressing the incomparable greatness and transcendence of God.

'*The blessed and only Ruler*', stresses His relation to the universe and world-rulers. He is Controller of all things. The scope of His authority is universal—the blessed and *only* Ruler, who has the right to do exactly as He pleases. His sovereignty is inherent, not delegated. Men may claim or be invested with honoured and honourable titles, but God alone is King over all kings and Lord over all lords. Every other sovereignty is under His supreme control.

'*Living in unapproachable light*' stresses His inaccessibility, except as He chooses to be accessible. He is inaccessible to mere human senses. Such are His majesty and holiness that no man could look on Him in His unveiled glory and live. He dwells in an atmosphere so rare that mortals cannot approach Him. But although we cannot approach the sun, we can walk in the sunshine. It is not that He is unapproachable, for there is a way of approach, but it is bloodstained.

> There is a way for man to rise
> To that sublime abode,

An offering and a sacrifice,
A Holy Spirit's energies,
An Advocate with God.

T. Binney

God our Saviour

'Teach slaves...to show that they can be fully trusted, so that in every way they will make the teaching about God our Saviour attractive' (Tit 2:9,10).

The word 'Saviour' holds a wealth of imagery. This title is peculiar to the pastoral epistles, but the idea pervades the whole of Scripture. The Greek word *soter* usually means deliverer. It was used of an emperor or conqueror who delivered his people from some calamity or conferred great benefits. God is our Saviour from sin and death and hell. He is 'the Saviour of all men, and especially of those who believe' (1 Tim 4:10), a statement that assures us of the *salvability* of all men, but not the *salvation* of all men. That requires the exercise of personal faith. He is the *potential* Saviour because He has provided salvation for all, but the *actual* Saviour only of those who believe.

'*God who richly provides us with everything* for our enjoyment' (1 Tim 6:17). Greek scholars point out that in the original of verse 17 there is a play on words that could be rendered: The *rich* are not to trust in uncertain *riches* but in God who *richly* provides everything for our enjoyment—for soul and body, for time and eternity.

Ours is a beneficent and lavish God who grants us, not a minimum of pleasure and gratification, but an abundance of riches—'everything' for soul and body, for time and eternity. Contrary to the teaching of the Gnostics of that day to which he had referred in 1 Timothy 4:3—'forbidding to marry and ordering them to abstain from certain foods, which God created to be received with thanksgiving'—we are not only to partake of them but *enjoy* them with gratitude to the Giver. Only sin can prevent our enjoyment of God's lavish provision.

The God whom Timothy and Titus loved was not only happy, sovereign, immortal, invisible, transcendent, but a lavish God who gives good things in abundance.

Paul is in effect saying to the young leaders, 'This is the kind of God on whom you can utterly rely and fully trust, and on whom you can with confidence lean in your service —a God whom you will find adequate for every emergency and sufficient for every need that will arise in your ministry that lies ahead.'

God the Son

Paul's faith was centred in the person and work of Jesus Christ. To him Christianity was Christ.

When he said, 'To me to live is Christ' (Phil 1:21), he was not employing poetic licence, but was simply stating a literal, conscious fact. Upon conversion and the absolute self-surrender to his Lord that accompanied it, the centre of his life had completely changed. Up till then life had been Paul, now it was Christ. Martin Luther's words in his *Table Talk* could well have been Paul's: 'Should anyone knock at my heart and say "Who lives here?", I should reply, "Not Martin Luther, but the Lord Jesus Christ"'.

Paul's version was 'I have been crucified with Christ and I no longer live, but Christ lives in me. The life I live in the body, I live by faith in the Son of God, who loved me and gave himself for me' (Gal 2:20). His entire personality and all his activities were under the sway of Christ and permeated by His presence. All that followed of ministry and sacrificial service found its source in this glorious fact. His life was a continuing appropriation of Christ to meet all his daily needs.

In his letter to Timothy, he charged him: 'Remember always, *as the centre of everything*, Jesus Christ . . . raised by

God from the dead' (2 Tim 2:8 in J. B. Phillips' translation).
He was not merely telling Timothy to focus his attention on
the fact and doctrine of the resurrection, or he would have
said, 'Remember that Jesus rose from the dead'. He was
directing him never to forget the Person who rose from the
dead, for He is in reality the centre of everything. Christianity *is* Christ. From that initial moment of revelation,
everything revolved around Christ as centre. Christ was
ever on his lips and in his heart.

Paul's preaching was centred on Christ. To the Corinthians he declared: 'I resolved to know nothing while I was
with you except Jesus Christ and him crucified' (1 Cor 2:2).
Concerning his ministry in Corinth, the record runs: 'Paul
devoted himself exclusively to preaching, testifying to the
Jews that Jesus was the Christ' (Acts 18:5). In Thessalonica,
'On three Sabbath days he reasoned with them from the
Scriptures, explaining and proving that the Christ had to
suffer and rise from the dead. "This Jesus I am proclaiming
to you is the Christ", he said' (Acts 17:2,3).

These and other similar passages demonstrate the central
place he accorded to Christ both in life and ministry.

The lordship of Christ was a constant emphasis of the
Apostle. As he used the term in his writings, the title 'Lord'
uniformly denotes Christ. In his initial surrender he
embraced without reservation Christ's lordship and absolute
mastery of his life. This was implied in his question, 'What
shall I do *Lord*?' With quick spiritual insight he realized
that the purpose of Christ's death and resurrection went far
beyond the mere salvation of the believer from judgement,
but had in view the recognition of His lordship. He later
expressed it in these words: 'For this very reason, Christ
died and returned to life *so that he might be the Lord* of both
the dead and the living' (Rom 14:9). It was his constant joy
to press for recognition of 'the crown rights of the
Redeemer'.

It is to Paul that we owe the phrase that appears so often

and in so many contexts in his writings—'in Christ'. The idea behind the phrase, as he uses it, appears to be that just as the sea is the sphere or element in which fish live, so Christians live in the sphere or element of Christ, joined to Him by an invisible yet inseparable bond. Every spiritual blessing is ours because we are 'in Christ' in a living, vital union (Eph 1:3). A study of the occurrences of the phrase will uncover a rich vein of truth.

The greatest Christological passage in the New Testament comes from his pen—Philippians 2:5–11. In this paragraph he first affirms *the humiliation of the Son of God*, calling attention to His pre-existence, incarnation and crucifixion. He then unfolds *the exaltation of the Son of Man*—honoured and worshipped by all creation. In view of these glorious truths, he exhorts, 'Let this mind be in you which was also in Christ Jesus' (v.5).

God the Holy Spirit

Shortly before His death, in His Upper Room discourse, our Lord had more to say to His men about the Holy Spirit and His ministry than in all His previous teaching. But when speaking on that very theme, He made this rather mysterious statement: 'I have much more to say to you, more than you can now bear. But when he, the Spirit of truth, comes, he will guide you into all truth' (Jn 16:12,13). It was principally through Paul that this further revelation was communicated. It is not surprising, therefore, to find his writings studded with references to the Holy Spirit.

In Paul's own experience the Spirit played a very important part. Immediately after his conversion he was filled with the Holy Spirit (Acts 9:17) so it is not surprising to find him exhorting the Ephesian Christians—and us as well—to be filled with the Spirit (Eph 5:18). His call to service and commissioning were through the Spirit (Acts 13:1,4). He was guided through the restraint or constraint of the Spirit

(Acts 16:6,7). He depended on the Spirit for power in preaching (1 Cor 2:4). The Spirit warned him of impending dangers (Acts 21:4,11–14).

He emphasized the working of the Spirit in his preaching and teaching. As Administrator of the Church, the Spirit took the initiative in the selection of elders (Acts 20:28), and His was the authorizing voice at the first Church Council (Acts 15:28). When Paul met the small group of men at Ephesus, his first probing question was, 'Did you receive the Holy Spirit when you believed?' (Acts 19:2), and then he led them into the experience (v.6).

The varying names he uses for the Spirit highlight different facets of His ministry: the Spirit of power and love and of self-discipline (2 Tim 1:7); Spirit of faith (2 Cor 4:13); Spirit of wisdom (Eph 1:17); Spirit of holiness (Rom 1:4); Spirit of promise (Eph 1:13); Spirit of adoption (Rom 8:15); Spirit of life (Rom 8:2).

He taught that both justification and sanctification are the results of His working (1 Cor 6:11; 2 Thess 2:13). He inspires worship (Phil 3:3). He indwells (1 Cor 3:16), and strengthens us (Rom 14:17). He helps in prayer (Rom 8:26,27), and dispenses joy (1 Thess 1:6). He promotes and maintains the unity of the Church (Eph 4:4).

It was the Spirit's ministry that gave Paul victory over the flesh—the fallen nature that he and we received from Adam. It is only by the Spirit that we can 'put to death the misdeeds of the body' (Rom 8:12,13). It is the Holy Spirit's delight to produce in the life of the yielded believer the spiritual fruits listed in Galatians 5:22–23.

Spiritual gifts

Paul taught that the Holy Spirit distributed various spiritual gifts, so essential to the leadership, expansion and up-building of the Church. These gifts or special qualifications are valuable and to be desired only when they serve practical ends—the edification of the Church. To be effective every kind of ministry must be inspired and made efficient by the Holy Spirit, and these gifts are God's gracious provision to this end. Since we fight a supernatural foe, only supernatural weapons will suffice.

Two words are used of these gifts—*pneumatika*, something from the Spirit, and *charismata*, gifts of grace (1 Cor 12:1,4). Spiritual gifts are sovereignly bestowed on individuals as gifts for service in the Church. They are distinct from natural gifts, although they often operate through them. There is some gift for every believer (1 Cor 12:7), not merely for a spiritual elite, but individual gifts may not be claimed as of right (1 Cor 12:11). To be profitable they must be exercised in love (1 Cor 13:1,2).

No gift is to be despised, but some are more valuable than others (1 Cor 12:31; 14:5). Paul urges the primacy of prophecy, as the ministry of the Word is the gift of greatest value. We are warned that spiritual gifts can atrophy through neglect (1 Tim 4:14) and need to be stimulated (2 Tim 1:6).

These gifts are not given for the mere joy or aggrandisement of the believer or even for the sake of his own spiritual life, but primarily for ministry to others (1 Cor 14:12), and to bring saints to spiritual maturity (Eph 4:11–13). It is significant that not one of the gifts refers directly to character, all are gifts for service.

Few discover their gifts at the beginning of their Christian lives, and they frequently lie dormant until a specific occasion reveals them. They are often more evident to others than to ourselves, but we can be sure that at the right time God will reveal the gift or combination of gifts that are necessary for fulfilling the ministry in the Body of Christ that He assigns to us.

In 1 Corinthians chapters 12 to 14 the Apostle warns the Corinthians against the unworthy use of spiritual gifts, and lays down guidelines for their exercise in the Church.

5

Paul's Doctrine of the Cross

> I resolved to know nothing while I was with you except Jesus
> Christ and him crucified (1 Cor 2:2).

In Paul's view, the Christian faith revolved around the twin
centres of Calvary and Pentecost, those two well-attested
historical events. At his conversion the real significance of
the Cross dawned on his soul, and immediately afterwards
he experienced the blessings of the Holy Spirit that Pentecost had brought. Henceforth his attitude was consistently
expressed in the words: 'May I never boast except in the
cross of our Lord Jesus Christ, through which the world has
been crucified to me, and I to the world' (Gal 6:14).

Calvary was a magnificent demonstration of sacrificial
love, but without the dynamic released by the Holy Spirit at
Pentecost it would have been stillborn. Pentecost was the
necessary complement of Calvary. The descent of the Spirit
made actual in the experience of believers what Calvary
had made possible.

Among many facets of the death of our Lord, Paul
emphasized the following:

A propitiation for our sins

'Being justified freely by his grace through the redemption

that is in Christ Jesus: Whom God hath set forth *to be a propitiation* through faith in his blood' (Rom 3:25 KJV). John adds his witness: '*He is the propitiation for our sins*, and not for ours only, but also for the sins of the whole world' (1 Jn 2:2 KJV).

This thought is absolutely basic to Christianity, and figured prominently in Paul's preaching and teaching. God has declared his implacable wrath against sin, and His justice demands that all sin will meet with its just retribution. Christ's death, viewed as a propitiation, quenched God's wrath by bearing, and bearing away—obliterating—our sins, so that they no longer stand as a barrier between us and Him.

Deliverance from sin

'Christ gave himself for us *to redeem us from all wickedness* and to purify for himself a people that are his very own, eager to do what is good' (Tit 2:14).

Although Christ's death secured for us full justification from all sin, it would have failed of its full purpose had it left us victims of sin's tyranny. It is not sufficient for a festering sore to be superficially healed over, if the internal source of infection is not dealt with. Its poison would continue to circulate in the bloodstream. The perfect atoning sacrifice of our Lord does not leave us in such a tragic plight.

The purpose of Christ's death, Paul contends, is both positive and negative. Our Redeemer not only bought us back, but He emancipated us from the enslavement of sin. He paid the costly ransom price in crimson drops of precious blood (1 Pet 1:18,19). By His victory over the devil, over sin and over death, He gained for us potential deliverance from sin of every kind—*all* wickedness—conscious or unconscious, disreputable or respectable, sins of the flesh or sins of the mind.

If it is asked whether this emancipation from sin's tyranny

takes place in a moment or over a period of time, the paradoxical answer is both! According to Paul's teaching, the *crisis* leading to deliverance may occur when the Christian, conscious of his inability to free himself, claims his part in the delivering power of the Cross. Then follows the *process* of sanctification in which the Holy Spirit makes the potential actual in experience. 'For we know that our old self was crucified with him so that . . . we should no longer be slaves to sin' (Rom 6:6).

Once the crisis is over, the process of sanctification accelerates and continues so long as Christ's Lordship is recognized in actuality. In this process, the Holy Spirit progressively removes whatever hinders our being transformed into the image of Christ, and leads us into the experience of Romans 6:18: 'You have been set free from sin and have become slaves to righteousness'.

Dedication to Christ

'He died for all, that those who live *should no longer live for themselves* but for him who died for them and was raised again' (2 Cor 5:15).

Such amazing grace and love as was shown on the Cross demands a reciprocal response—the shifting of life's centre from self to Christ. The acceptance of Christ's propitiation logically means the end of the old life of self-pleasing, and finding a new centre in Him. To live for self after having taken His costly salvation is to rob Him of the fruit of His passion.

Life is now viewed in two dimensions—'hitherto' and 'henceforth'. Hitherto self has been the central point of reference. Henceforth time, talents, friends, possessions, recreations are all under His control. Contrary to expectation, such an embracing of the Cross of Christ, such a complete surrender to Him as Lord, brings a liberty that can be experienced in no other way. 'Through Christ Jesus the law of the Spirit of life set me free from the law of sin and death' (Rom 8:2).

'Whoso looketh on the white side of Christ's cross, and takes it up handsomely', said Samuel Rutherford, 'will find it just such a burden as wings are to a bird'.

Detachment from the present age

'The Lord Jesus Christ . . . gave himself for our sins *to rescue us from the present evil age*' (Gal 1:4). Paul here indicates that Christ's death was not merely a noble example of heroism and an expression of love, although it was both, but it was essentially a sacrifice for sin. It had also a subsidiary purpose, that of rescuing us from the power and corrupting influence of this present world or age.

The term 'world' or 'age' refers to this evil era from the viewpoint of time and change. It is hastening to its close and has in it nothing of eternal value. Paul shared his Master's view of this age when He said, 'If the world hates you, keep in mind that it hated me first. If you belonged to the world, it would love you as its own. As it is, you do not belong to the world' (Jn 15:18,19).

Jesus had more than physical detachment from the world in view, for He prayed, 'My prayer is not that you take them out of the world but that you protect them from the evil one' (Jn 17:15). We are to detach ourselves morally and spiritually from the world while we are in it, but it must be *insulation*, not isolation, living in a holy ghetto. Believers are the salt of the earth, but salt can exercise its antiseptic and pungent influence only when there is contact. It is when we can say with Paul, 'the world has been crucified to me, and I to the world' (Gal 6:14), that we can make our greatest impact on the evil age in which we live. Compromise with the spirit of the age shortcircuits the power of the Spirit, and thus neutralizes our spiritual influence.

Christ's enthronement

'For this very reason, Christ died and returned to life *so that he might be the Lord* of both the dead and the living' (Rom 14:9).

Could words more simply and explicitly state the ultimate purpose of the Cross? In the previous passages we have been considering Christ's purpose *for us* in His death. Here the focus is on its purpose *for Himself*—to obtain complete sovereignty over the lives for which He died, in time and in eternity.

Peter proclaimed the indisputable fact—'He is Lord of all'—but the Lord yearns for our spontaneous recognition of that fact. Too many Christians are only too willing to accept all the benefits of His salvation, but are reluctant to bow to His full sovereignty. Paul envisages the day when recognition of His sovereignty will be universal—'every knee shall bow in heaven and on earth' (Phil 2:10), but our Master longs that before that day, there will be a *voluntary coronation* rather than a compulsory recognition.

Ideally that coronation day should be at conversion, but if Christ's claims to Lordship are not fully realized at that time, then He should be enthroned as soon as those rights are recognized.

William Borden, the young American millionaire who died on his way to the mission field, took this step in the following words:

> Lord Jesus, I take my hands off as far as my life is concerned. I put Thee on the throne of my heart. Change, cleanse me, use me as Thou shalt choose.

6

Paul's Exemplary Prayer Life

Paul was a leader by appointment and by universal recognition
and acceptance. He had many mighty forces in this ministry.
His conversion, so conspicuous and radical, was a great force, a
perfect magazine of aggressive and defensive warfare. His call
to the apostleship was clear, luminous and convincing. But
these forces were not the divinest energies which brought forth
the largest results to his ministry. Paul's course was more
distinctly shaped and his career rendered more powerfully
successful by prayer than by any other force.[22]

To read Paul's letters is to discover the supremely important place he conceived prayer to occupy in the life of a
spiritual leader. Nowhere does he betray the quality of his
own spiritual life more clearly than in his prayers. We should
be deeply grateful, therefore, for the self-revelation in the
prayers that stud his letters. He is at his best in his prayers.

It is obvious that Paul did not regard prayer as supple-
mental, but as fundamental; not something to be added to
his work, but the very source out of which his work was born.
He was a man of action because he was a man of prayer. It
was his prayer probably even more than his preaching that
produced the kind of leaders we meet in his letters.

It is significant that nowhere does he argue the case for
prayer. He does not even make an attempt to explain it, but
assumes it to be the natural and normal expression of the

81

spiritual life. He does not have to fret over failure to meet his prayer obligations as we often do, and he never seemed to be plagued with a condemning heart that robbed him of his confidence in prayer (1 Jn 5:14, 15). He regarded nothing as being beyond the reach of prayer.

> Prayer is the Christian's vital breath,
> The Christian's native air,
> His watchword at the gate of death;
> He enters heaven with prayer.

> *J. Montgomery*

While Paul's recorded prayers are not formal or obviously structured, they are anything but slovenly and haphazard. It is clear that they did not just happen, but were the outcome of careful thought. A study of them will reveal a depth of adoration, a height of thanksgiving and a breadth of intercession that leave one awed.

At times he breaks out into doxology when his whole soul flames up to heaven like incense on the altar fire. At other times his prayer is quiet and contemplative. An old man of God asserted that our prayers are cold, dry and repetitious because there is so little of Christ in them. But no such charge could be preferred against Paul. To stand at his prison door and listen to the prayers that ascended there, and are recorded in his letters, is to be reminded of his Master's prayer in John 17.

While it is true that prayer cannot be analysed, there is a sense in which it can be divided into constituent elements. A study of Paul's prayers reveals a remarkable balance. The elements that go to make up a balanced prayer life are easily discernible. *Worship and adoration* are prominent— prostrating the soul before God in adoring contemplation, paying Him the reverence and honour that are His due. In his worship Paul ascribed praise to God for what He was in Himself as well as for what He has done.

His prayers were replete with *thanksgiving and praise*—the appreciative acknowledgment of the benefits and blessings God gives, whether to ourselves or to others.

Confession of sin had no place in the life of our Lord, but that was not so in the case of the Apostle. In his letters and addresses there is an acute sense of sin. 'I know that nothing good lives in me, that is, in my sinful nature. For I have the desire to do what is good, but I cannot carry it out . . . the evil I do not want to do—this I keep on doing' (Rom 7:18, 19).

Next comes *petition*—bringing before our heavenly Father who 'knows what we have need of before we ask him', our daily and recurring needs. It is striking to note the priorities in prayer established by our Lord in His pattern prayer. It is half way through before there is any mention of personal needs. The first part is taken up with God, and our relations with Him. A similar proportion can be discerned in the Apostle's prayers. He was not an ascetic who had no needs, but they did not come first in his order of priorities. Most of his prayers are concerned with the needs of others. But he did not neglect to bring his own daily needs, both temporal and spiritual, before the Lord in confident expectation of their supply.

The greater part of his prayers is occupied with *intercession,* the personal presentation of the needs of others at the throne of grace. This is the unselfish side of prayer. He was ever praying for his converts and churches. Intercession does not have in view the overcoming of the reluctance of God, but the confident pleading of the merits of Christ on behalf of others who may often be in a less privileged position. Intercession was the life-blood of Paul's experience, and a study of his recorded prayers reveals the things he considered most desirable in the spiritual development of his flock.

It was the experience of Henry Martyn that at times of spiritual dryness and depression—and who does not have such experiences—he often found 'a delightful revival in the act of praying for others, for their conversion or sanctification, or prosperity in the work of the Lord'.[23]

Characteristics of Paul's prayers

In referring to men who had been prominent in evangelistic and revival work in his book, *Prayer and Praying Men*, E. M. Bounds says, 'They were not leaders because of brilliancy of thought, because they were exhaustless in resources, because of their magnificent culture or native endowment, but *because of the power of prayer they could command the power of God*.' This gives in a nutshell the secret of Paul's amazing leadership. While he possessed all the qualities of a leader in rich measure, he renounced dependence on them, and through prayer and communion allowed his life to be a channel for the distribution of divine power.

Consider some other characteristics of his prayers that are a model for a leader who carries spiritual responsibility.

They were *unceasing*. 'Night and day I constantly remember you in my prayers' (2 Tim 1:3). This obviously does not mean that he did nothing else. He used the word in the sense of 'incessant, ever-recurring'. An incessant cough is not one that never stops, but one that constantly recurs. When Paul's mind was free of other concerns, be it day or night, his heart turned to prayer as the needle to the magnetic pole. This was not the language of exaggeration. Perhaps the reason we find such constancy difficult to envisage is that our minds are so secular and engrossed with things of less importance. To Paul everything was a cause for prayer or praise.

They were *strenuous*. 'I want you to know how much I am struggling for you and for those at Laodicea' (Col 2:1). This is an aspect of praying that is all too little experienced. Prayer is not merely a comfortable, dreamy reverie. There is a restful aspect of prayer, but this is something very different. 'Prayer is never meant to be *indolently easy,* however simple and reliant it may be,' said Bishop Moule.

Prayer regarded as conflict or struggle includes the ideas of toil and strife. Paul knew that to really pray would arouse mighty opposition in the unseen realm. The word 'struggle' is associated with 'the good fight of faith' (1 Tim 6:12). It is one of the most vivid and strong figures of speech, and from it we derive our word 'agonize'. Paul uses it elsewhere of an athlete competing in the arena (1 Cor 9:25); a soldier battling for his life (1 Tim 6:12); a labourer toiling until he is weary (Col 1:29). How pallid and tepid do our prayers appear in comparison! Paul's prayers often became a groan (2 Cor 5:2–4).

> How have I knelt with arms of my aspiring
> Lifted all night in irresponsive air,
> Dazed and amazed with overmuch desiring,
> Blank with the utter agony of prayer.
>
> Shame on the flame so dying to an ember!
> Shame on the reed so lightly overset!
> Yes, I have seen Him, can I not remember?
> Yes, I have known Him, and shall Paul forget?
>
> *F. W. H. Myers*

They were *submissive.* Once he had discovered it, he was content with the will of God. There are some who contend that to pray, 'If it be Thy will', is a negation of faith. Granted that it may be so, this is not always necessarily the case. Jesus prayed, 'Father, if it be possible, let this cup pass from me'. Paul believed in a wisdom and will beyond his own, and when the Father's will became plain, he cordially accepted a divine refusal, and counted on the sufficiency of divine grace to enable him to triumph.

'Three times I pleaded with the Lord to take it (the thorn)

away from me. But he said to me, "My grace is sufficient for you, for my power is made perfect in weakness". Therefore I will boast all the *more gladly* about my weaknesses, so that Christ's power may rest on me' (2 Cor 12:8, 9).

His prayers were *confident*. The seeming impossibility of a situation did not daunt him or discourage prayer. To a man who constantly lived in the realm of the supernatural and was in constant communion with the Omnipotent God, nothing was impossible save that which was beyond the scope of the divine will. When he prayed, he confidently expected the supernatural intervention of God if that were necessary. He knew no circumstances in which prayer was not appropriate.

A typical example of this confidence is recorded in Acts 27:23–26. 'Last night', he wrote, 'an angel of the God whose I am and whom I serve stood beside me and said, "Do not be afraid, Paul. You must stand trial before Caesar; and God has graciously given you the lives of all who sail with you." So keep up your courage, men, for I have faith in God that it will happen just as he told me.'

His prayers were *covetous*, that is to say, he was not unwilling to ask for anything. We can find encouragement in the fact that even the great Apostle, one of the greatest exponents of the art of prayer, was not self-sufficient. He was often made conscious of his inadequacy in this area, and felt the need of the aid of the Holy Spirit. 'In the same way, the Spirit helps us in our weakness. *We do not know what we ought to pray*, but the Spirit himself intercedes for us with groans that words cannot express' (Rom 8:26).

He *coveted the prayers of his fellows*. Indeed, he regarded their prayers for himself, not as a desirable extra, but as a determining factor in his ministry. His letters contain many pleas for prayer fellowship, e.g. 'For I know that through your prayers and the help given by the Spirit of Jesus Christ, what has happened to me will turn out for my deliverance' (Phil 1:19). Thus Paul and his converts supported each other in prayer.

He regarded prayer as *a co-operative effort* within the church. 'Brothers, pray for us', he asked the newly-converted Thessalonian believers (1 Thess 5:25). To the Corinthians he wrote: 'On him we have set our hope that he will continue to deliver us, as you help us by your prayers' (2 Cor 1:10, 11). He craved the prayers of others for such matters as bold utterance and open doors: 'Pray also for me, that whenever I open my mouth, words may be given me' (Eph 6:19); 'Pray for us that God may open a door for our message' (Col 4:3).

His prayers were *strategic*. There were no trivialities. He prays for things that are central to the divine purpose and to the growth and maturity of the Church. His prayers reveal the factors which he deemed of paramount importance.

In the prayer of Colossians 2:1–3 Paul sums up some of the greatest needs of young converts and emerging churches. He is here praying for people he had never seen, a fact which should encourage us in praying for missionary situations. He prayed for *encouragement,* 'that they may be encouraged in heart' in the face of strong temptation to discouragement; for *unity* in the midst of Satanic attempts to promote division, 'that they may be united in love'; for *assurance,* 'so that they might have the full riches of complete understanding'; for *knowledge* of the mystery of God, namely Christ'. Such prayers form a model for the Christian leader.

His prayers were *Spirit-inspired*. He counted on the Holy Spirit to complement his weakness and inadequacy (Rom 8:26, 27). It is the Spirit's delight to aid those entrusted with spiritual leadership in this vital aspect of ministry.

We all labour under a threefold handicap, and the Spirit aids us in each area. First, *the iniquity of our hearts* that discourages prayer and brings condemnation. The Spirit leads us to appropriate the cleansing power of the blood of Christ, that mighty solvent for all sin. Secondly, *the ignorance of our minds*. The Spirit knows the mind and will of God, and will communicate it to the obedient and receptive heart. He will impart the conviction that the prayer is or is not the will of God. Thirdly, *the infirmity* of our bodies. The body can indeed be a 'clog' to prayer. The Spirit will help us to rise above adverse physical conditions whether of health or climate.

In the area of prayer, it is important to be alert, lest we have slipped into unconscious and unintentional independence of the Holy Spirit, for we are always to 'pray in the Spirit', as Paul exhorts in Ephesians 6:18.

7

Paul as a Communicator

Without doubt one of the most potent elements in Paul's leadership was his ability to communicate divine truth powerfully and convincingly. Most popular leaders possess this ability.

In World War II, Adolph Hitler and Winston Churchill were the outstanding figures. Hitler's pronouncements were not always worthy of note, but he spoke wisely when he claimed: 'The power which has set in motion the greatest avalanches of power in politics and religion has been from the beginning of time the magic of the spoken word.'[24] His own frenzied speeches vindicated his viewpoint.

On the other hand, Winston Churchill led and galvanized the free world into action as much by his measured, intrepid, inspiring speeches at critical moments, as by his great political and military gifts.

Paul was essentially a preacher, a flaming herald of the Good News. If preaching is gauged by the results it achieves, then Paul was preacher *par excellence*. He earned the right to exhort Timothy, 'Preach the Word; be prepared in season and out of season' (2 Tim 4:2).

But he laid no claim to superior human powers of oratory. 'When I came to you, brothers, I did not come with eloquence or superior wisdom as I proclaimed to you the testimony about God' (1 Cor 2:1). His reliance was on the

Holy Spirit, not on worldly powers of persuasion. 'My message and my preaching were not with wise and persuasive words, but with a demonstration of the Spirit's power' (1 Cor 2:4).

In keeping with the flexibility of his mind, his method of communication was adapted to the occasion.

At times it was *polemical*. He satisfied his hearers' reason by presenting incontrovertible proofs. 'Saul grew more and more powerful and baffled the Jews living in Damascus by proving that Jesus is the Christ' (Acts 9:22). He did not adopt evasive tactics when confronted with a difficult argument, nor was he an intellectual coward, afraid to defend his beliefs. His pulpit was no coward's castle.

His presentation of truth was carefully reasoned. 'So he reasoned in the synagogue with the Jews and the God-fearing Greeks, as well as in the market-place day by day with those who happened to be there' (Acts 17:17). His objective was not merely to win the argument, but to win his opponents for Christ.

It was *persuasive*. He did not simply present cold facts with convincing logic and leave it there, but accompanied his appeal with warm entreaty. He delighted to beseech rather than to command or warn. 'Every Sabbath he reasoned in the synagogue, trying to persuade Jews and Greeks' (Acts 18:4).

He believed in a coming judgement; that God was not merely an indulgent grandfather but a God of judgement who hated sin with an implacable hatred and who must purge it from the universe. This belief lent urgency to his pleadings. 'Since, then, we know what it is to fear the Lord, we try to persuade men' (2 Cor 5:11). And in this art he was singularly successful. 'Paul entered the synagogue and spoke boldly there for three months, arguing persuasively about the kingdom of God' (Acts 19:8).

His preaching was often *didactic*—adapted to meet the special needs of his hearers—for he was both teacher and preacher. Two periods of extended preaching and teaching are recorded—three years in the School of Tyrannus, and eighteen months in Corinth (Acts 19:9 and 18:11 RSV). He frequently adopted the method of question and answer to clinch his teachings. Since men must have a factual basis if their faith is to be intelligent, he painstakingly instructed them in the things of God.

His teaching method was *versatile*. There was nothing stereotyped in his approach. He suited his message to his audience, as his address at Athens attests. While the content of his message remained constant, he sought common ground with those he addressed, whether Jewish congregations in the synagogues, Greek philosophers at the Acropolis, or pagan crowds at Lystra. He was equally at home with governors and officials, philosophers and theologians.

As to the *tone* of his preaching, Paul could not be charged with 'the curse of a dry-eyed Christianity'. 'Remember', he exhorted the Ephesians, 'that for three years I never stopped warning you night and day with tears' (Acts 20:31). There is something moving in manly tears. 'As I have often told you before and now say again even with tears, many live as enemies of the cross of Christ' (Phil 3:18). Paul was not ashamed of his tears.

Paul's communication technique

Paul's address on Mars Hill, recorded in Acts 17:22–34, is regarded by some as his greatest failure in communication. Their interpretation is that in addressing his distinguished and erudite Athenian audience, instead of preaching 'Christ and him crucified', he pandered to the philosophers and so lost his opportunity. In support of their position they quote his affirmation to the Corinthians, 'I resolved to know nothing while I was with you except Jesus Christ and him crucified' (1 Cor 2:2), as reflecting his determination to change his approach.

Others, however, view it as one of his greatest messages, and allege that his approach could not be improved on. S. M. Zwemer called it 'a marvel of tactful and powerful preaching'. F. B. Meyer affirmed that 'for its grace and intellectual sequence, grandeur of conception and range, stately march of eloquent words, it stands alone'.[25] Paul would undoubtedly be disappointed at the reception accorded to his message by the majority, but was it Paul who failed, or the Athenians?

Whichever view is taken, this address gives helpful insight into his communication techniques. In it he displayed his amazing versatility in 'becoming all things to all men'—an intellectual to the intellectuals—'so that by all possible means' he might save some (1 Cor 9:22). In this he was successful.

Let us analyse the results of his preaching (vv. 32–34) which even Alexander Maclaren dismissed as 'little less than naught':

Some sneered—ironical mocking, cynical disdain.

Some temporized—'we want to hear you again on this subject'—they procrastinated in indecision.

Some believed—'a few men became followers of Paul and believed'. A group of men embraced the message.

'Among them was Dionysius, a member of the Areopagus' (Acts 17:32, 33). The Areopagus was the College of twelve judges who made Athens famous. A modern equivalent would be the conversion of a judge of the United States Supreme Court. Suppose Chief Justice Burger of the U.S. Supreme Court professed faith under the preaching of Billy Graham, would that address be considered a failure? The conversion of Dionysius was a parallel. How often are leading jurists converted? Paul himself said that not many wise were chosen by God. The tradition is that Dionysius later became Bishop of Corinth.

Another convert was Damaris, a foreign and well-educated aristocratic woman. It has been suggested that she was probably a God-fearer who had heard Paul preach in the synagogue. 'And a number of others', is the closing remark. Not a bad catch for one address to a group of mentally sated intellectuals! Many preachers today would be happy to experience such a failure.

One point to be borne in mind in assessing Paul's message is that it was interrupted and cut short, and he had no opportunity to complete it, so we have no idea of its full content. Nor need we conclude that the greatly condensed report in Acts comprising only 257 words is all that he said. The content of his message is summarized in verse 18: 'They said this because Paul was preaching the good news about Jesus and the resurrection'.

There is much for the Christian leader to learn from his approach. Several points should be noted.

He adapted himself to his audience. In addressing the people of Pisidian Antioch, he appealed almost entirely to the Old Testament Scriptures with which they were familiar (Acts 13:14, 15). In speaking to the peasants at Lystra, however, he expressed similar thoughts in different language. He used no Old Testament references, for they were ignorant of them, but appealed to the beneficence of God (Acts 14:15–18).

At Athens, when addressing Greek philosophers, he established a rapport by quoting their own poets, and gave a biblical philosophy of their history, following up with a reasoned discourse about the nature of the Godhead.

His flexibility of mind in thus adapting his message to the differing groups illustrated what he meant by 'becoming all things to all men'. The lesson for the missionary is that he should study the literature and culture of the people so that he will be able to speak on their wave-length, especially to the leaders or potential leaders of the group.

Paul's conciliatory prelude to his address is a model for emulation. With inimitable tact and courtesy, he introduced his subject by complimenting them on the obvious religious interest manifested in the proliferation of altars around the city. He did not begin by having a tilt at their idols. That would come later after rapport had been established. Nor did he quote Jewish references with which they would be unfamiliar.

Neither did he come down to the level of his philosophy-oriented hearers, as though Christianity was just another philosophy. Instead, he endeavoured to find a point in their current beliefs to which he could attach his own message. Because he was out to win them and not an intellectual argument, he limited himself to comment on one inscription on an altar which had caught his eye. He had his point of contact! *'To an unknown God'*. With great temerity Paul said, 'Now what you worship as something unknown I am going to proclaim to you' (Acts 17:23).

He first emphasized points in common rather than of difference in order to gain their attention, but having achieved this end, he launched into a polemic against idolatry. His courtesy did not lead him to condone error.

Dr S. M. Zwemer points out that while it is true Paul recognized all the good he could find in Athens, far from pandering to their Attic pride, he laid the axe to it. He challenged them on five points:

They declared themselves to have sprung from the soil. In verse 24 Paul asserts that GOD made the world and all things.

They pointed to the Acropolis and its beautiful architecture. Paul said, 'God who made the world and everything in it ... does not live in temples built by hands' (v. 24).

They felt infinitely superior to the barbarians, but Paul asserts, 'From one man he made every nation of men, that they should inhabit the whole earth (v. 26).

They prided themselves on their chronology and antiquity, but Paul contended that it was God and not Herodotus who 'determined the times set for them, and the exact places where they should live' (v. 26).

The vaunted 'Golden Age of Pericles' was only evidence

of ignorance which God had graciously overlooked (v. 30).

Thus Paul routed the exclusive, pantheistic, materialistic Greeks and challenged them to repent.

'The whole address remains a model for those who seek in such circles to present the Christian way of faith, and a warning to those who, in misguided moments, have seen a virtue in crudity, and a loyalty to truth in a disrespect for the views, the habits of thought, the attitudes of intelligent people who fail in all points to follow them.'[26]

It should be said, however, that the Apostle did not confine himself to preaching formal sermons. In his contact with men and women of all classes he spontaneously and in colloquial language sought to lead them to Christ.

8

Paul the Missionary Leader

Writing of Paul in his role as a missionary prototype, Dr R. E. Speer, himself a notable missionary statesman, said, 'The first missionary marked out for all time the lines and principles of successful missionary work'. Whatever else he was, Paul was a missionary trail-blazer, leaving behind him a string of new churches pulsating with life. It is a significant fact that the greatest missionary advances of the last fifty years have followed the re-discovery or re-emphasis of Paul's missionary principles.

It is usually thought that Paul's Damascus Road experience was the root of his missionary enthusiasm, and in a sense this is true, but was he not already an ardent missionary for Judaism before his conversion? He wanted to be a missionary as well as a rabbi. Was this not at the root of his excessive persecuting zeal? Far from quenching this missionary passion, his conversion not only intensified it, but also altered its direction.

By teaching and example, Paul approximated the divine pattern more nearly than any missionary the world has seen. In him Christ possessed an instrument uniquely qualified, finely tuned and passionately devoted to the divine purpose. Indeed, He chose him precisely because He saw in him missionary raw material of unusual quality Other missionaries like David Livingstone have opened continents to the gospel. Paul opened a world.

His general call has been treated earlier, but we need to consider it further in relation to his subsequent missionary activities. On the Damascus Road, the Lord had intimated two things: (a) his ministry would be to distant lands; (b) it would be primarily to Gentiles (Acts 22:21; 26:16–18). Since Jesus was sent primarily to 'the lost sheep of the house of Israel', He had to leave the evangelization of the Gentiles to His followers, of whom Paul was to be the leader.

The universal character of the gospel was apprehended by the apostles only slowly. The first significant step in this direction was made when Peter overcame his narrow bigotry and went to the house of Cornelius, the Roman centurion (Acts 10:10–48). But subsequent events in Galatia proved that his prejudice had not been entirely dispelled (Gal 2:11–14). The conversion of the Gentiles on a world scale demanded someone with a broader mind and a larger heart than Peter. In Paul the Holy Spirit found a big-hearted and uniquely prepared instrument, but it was only gradually that he understood all the implications of his call. (*See* Acts 13:46; 18:6; 22:20, 21.)

It has been rightly contended that the call of the missionary today is not the revelation of a new purpose of God for his life, but the discovery of the purpose for which God sent him into the world; the culmination of a divine preparation that began before his birth. It was so with Paul. His career as a missionary was one of steady expansion. As he went forward in obedience, the plan of God for his life gradually began to take shape. His career was a demonstration of the fact that the blessing of God seems to rest in unusual measure on the frontiers of missionary advance.

The book of Acts was the world's first missionary manual, embodying both the history and philosophy of mission. It abounds in typical missionary scenes and events which afford valuable guidance for mission in every age. It reports failures as well as successes. It uncovers principles and indicates methods. It is God's commentary on problems encountered on most mission fields today. Covering as it does a period of thirty-three years, it is a graphic demonstration of what can be accomplished in a life-time by ordinary men and women.

Paul's methods

In considering the methods Paul employed as the human leader of the missionary enterprise, we note the following points:

1. In planning his strategy, he 'recognized that missions was a human task involving man in his total relationships and in his national, social and cultural identity. Thus he *sought to identify himself* as nearly as possible with the national and social strata of mankind in order to present the gospel intelligibly and acceptably.'[27] (See 1 Cor 9:16–23.) He accordingly adapted his tactics to his strategy.

2. Paul *did not confine his endeavours to any one stratum of society*. In this sense he was willing to be 'all things to all men'. He aimed to reach both the underprivileged and the influential. 'I am bound both to the Greeks and non-Greeks, both to the wise and the foolish. That is why I am so eager to preach the gospel also to you who are at Rome' (Rom 1:14, 15).

3. He by-passed villages and small towns in order to *concentrate on the more strategic large cities*, since they exercise most influence on the culture and habits of the people. Only thus could consistent growth be ensured.

4. Paul regarded *every home church* and its individual members as a *potential sending base*. He expected them to function as such in a comparatively short time. The Thessalonian church brought much joy to him in this regard. 'You became a model to all the believers in Macedonia and Achaia. The Lord's message rang out from you not only in Macedonia and Achaia—your faith has become known

everywhere' (1 Thess 1:7, 8).

5. He pursued *a policy of steady expansion,* but did not neglect a consolidating ministry in places already visited. (*See* Rom 15:20 and Acts 15:30.) 'Let us go back and visit the brothers in all the towns where we preached the word of the Lord and see how they are doing' (Acts 15:36). Letters were part of his pastoral care of the churches.

6. He engaged in consistent and *persistent itineration and personal evangelism.* He did not make the mistake of some leaders who counsel others to do what they themselves fail to do.

7. He *championed the cause of the Gentiles* against the legalists, and preached that all barriers are done away with in Christ. 'There is neither Jew nor Greek, slave nor free, male nor female, for you are all one in Christ Jesus' (Gal 3:28). Distinctions of race, class and sex were out.

8. He *denounced superficial methods of evangelism.* Mere evangelism did not satisfy him. His objective was to plant permanent churches among people responsive to the truth, and to lead believers into full maturity. He states the aim of his preaching succinctly in Colossians 1:28: 'We proclaim him, admonishing and teaching everyone with all wisdom, so that we may present everyone mature in Christ. To this end I labour, struggling with all his energy, which so powerfully works in me'.

When converts were won, he formed them into churches with a simple and flexible organization. 'They preached the news in that city (Antioch in Syria) and won a large number of disciples... Paul and Barnabas appointed elders for them in each church and, with prayer and fasting, committed them to the Lord in whom they had put their trust' (Acts 14:21–23).

9. He *preached a complete gospel*—the universality of sin and the certainty of judgement; the cruciality and sufficiency of the Cross; the resurrection and Second Coming of Christ. 'I declare to you today that I am innocent of the blood of all men. For I have not hesitated to proclaim to you the whole

will of God' (Acts 20:26–27). Even when in Thessalonica for only a short time, he presented the whole range of truth in embryo.

10. He *offered no financial baits,* but encouraged each church not only to be self-supporting but also generous in giving to others. When writing to the Corinthians, he cited the example of the Macedonian church which gave, 'even beyond their ability'. 'Just as you excel in everything', he encouraged them, 'in faith, in speech, in knowledge, in complete earnestness and in your love for us—see that you also excel in this grace of giving' (2 Cor 8:7).

11. He *practised the art of delegation.* While willing to carry a tremendous load of work and responsibility himself, he was too wise to assume too much responsibility for the churches. He knew how to delegate work and responsibility to others who, though less qualified, would grow and develop as they were entrusted with more responsibility. He thus kept on developing new leadership.

12. In saying 'Follow my example, as I follow the example of Christ' (1 Cor 11:1), Paul was setting a tremendously high standard, especially in the area of sacrificial service. He *set for his converts a standard no lower than he himself demonstrated.*

13. He *searched out and cultivated the friendship of promising young men* with leadership potential and schooled them to discipline themselves as good soldiers of Jesus Christ. 'Train yourself to be godly', he urged Timothy. 'For physical training is of some value, but godliness has value for all things, holding promise for both the present life and the life to come' (1 Tim 4:8).

14. When it was the wisest course in the circumstances, *he took no support* from the churches, but earned his living at tentmaking.

15. He had unbounded *confidence in the message of the gospel,* and in its power to transform individuals and communities (Rom 1:15).

16. He *had the spirit of the pioneer*. 'Our hope is that, as your faith continues to grow, our area of activity among you will greatly expand, so that we can preach the gospel in the regions beyond you. For we do not want to boast about work already done in another man's territory' (2 Cor 10:15–17).

To Paul, closed doors were not so much an obstacle as a challenge. He did not assume that because a door seemed to be closed it therefore meant that he should not attempt to enter it. Nor did he stand idly by and allow the devil to have an uncontested victory. He pushed the door to see if it would swing open (Acts 16:7), but accepted God's will without demur when it became clear, even when it went contrary to his desires.

Sometimes duty hindered him from fulfilling his objective. 'I planned many times to come to you (but have been prevented from doing so until now)' (Rom 1:13). Sometimes it was Satan who hindered: 'We wanted to come to you— certainly I, Paul, did again and again—but Satan stopped us' (1 Thess 2:17, 18). But usually he was successful in achieving his objective.

What a man! He richly earned Dean Farrar's assessment of him and his qualities: 'Paul, energetic as Peter and contemplative as John; Paul the hero of unselfishness; Paul the mighty champion of religious liberty; Paul, a greater preacher than Chrysostom, a greater missionary than Xavier, a greater reformer than Luther, a greater theologian than St Thomas Aquinas; Paul, the inspired apostle of the Gentiles, the slave of the Lord Jesus Christ.'[28]

Paul's disagreement with Barnabas

Missionaries are not exempt from the attacks of the adversary who is always on the alert to disturb harmony. Even godly men have their Achilles' heel, and Paul was no exception. The disagreement between him and Barnabas over John Mark holds salutary lessons for the would-be leader.

On their first missionary tour, John Mark defected and returned home from Perga. In Paul's eyes this was a serious dereliction of duty. When kind-hearted Barnabas wished to take John Mark with them on their second tour, Paul strongly objected. He considered the young man had neither the spirit nor the stamina for such a hazardous journey.

It was no mild disagreement that resulted. 'They had such a sharp disagreement that they parted company', runs the record (Acts 15:37–39). Barnabas's action smacked of nepotism, for John Mark was his nephew. He was caught in a clash of loyalties, and opted in favour of his relative. In the heat of the argument he became obstinate and Paul was intransigent. They reached an impasse, and there is no record that they prayed together about it. Instead, they reached the unhappy solution of going their different ways.

In retrospect it seems that there were elements of right in both viewpoints. Barnabas felt that the young man should be given the benefit of a second chance and that he would ultimately make good. He proved to be right. Paul thought more of the success of their mission and felt it was an unwarranted risk to take a team member who would be likely to defect again when the going got difficult. His reasoning is not difficult to follow.

Sir William Ramsay maintains that history marches with Paul, not Barnabas, for he and not Barnabas received the blessing of the Antioch church. On the other hand, Barnabas's optimistic conviction of the salvability of the young man proved well-founded, and Paul later wrote to Timothy: 'Get Mark and bring him with you, because he is helpful to me in my ministry' (2 Tim 4:11). This was the mark of a big man, a true leader.

The lesson proved salutary to Mark and his eyes were opened to his character defect, which doubtless threw him back on God's help.

The quarrel cannot be justified or condoned, but God 'turned the curse into a blessing'. The end result was the creation of two effective preaching teams. The quarrel was no fruit of the Spirit, but once again 'where sin increased, grace increased all the more' (Rom 5:20).

Such a situation is an ever-present possibility in Christian work—differences of opinion issuing in prayerless argument that results in a breach of fellowship. 'These things were written for our instruction'.

9

Paul's Views and Convictions

It is written: 'I believed, therefore I have spoken.' With the same spirit of faith we also believe and therefore speak (2 Cor 4:13).

Each one should be fully convinced in his own mind (Rom 14:5).

An open mind and a tolerant attitude are highly extolled in intellectual circles, and rightly so, provided the terms of reference are right. But there is an openness of mind and tolerance that is simply spinelessness.

On many subjects it is quite right to suspend judgement, e.g. matters that are morally neutral; or speculative interpretations of Scripture on which there is no clear word; or political or other issues on which alternative views are justified.

But there are some matters on which it is right to have a closed mind. When a Christian, after thorough thought and scriptural research has arrived at settled conclusions, he is right to maintain his settled convictions. Does a student of mathematics have an open mind whether two plus two make four? This does not mean that one must not be ready to consider other indisputable facts. That would merit the charge of obscurantism. But he will require incontrovertible evidence to make him change his mind. In the Christian life, we must work our way towards settled convictions as an anchorage in the restless sea of life.

'A conviction is a strong belief on the ground of satis-factory evidence, without any implication of previous error ...also a proposition going to make up such a belief' (Webster). Opinions cost us only breath, but convictions often cost life itself. We are all prolific in opinions, but few fight their way through to strong convictions. Some confuse prejudices with convictions, but prejudice only makes us bigots. We must arrive at certitude on the basic facts of our faith.

Like every strong leader, Paul cherished strong convic-tions, convictions that were like steel, strong and durable. He had unshakable beliefs concerning God and man, life and death, this world and the next. These lent colour and authority to his leadership. People love to follow a believer who believes his beliefs.

'It is not a preacher's wisdom but his conviction which imparts itself to others. Real flame kindles another flame. Men with convictions will speak and will be heard...No amount of reading or intellectual brilliance will take the place of thorough conviction and sincerity'.[29]

Convictions are not the product of reason and research alone. In his *Thoughts,* Pascal wrote, 'The heart has reasons that reason does not know. It is the heart that feels God, not the reason. There are truths that are felt and truths that are proved, for we know the truth not only by reason but by the intuitive conviction which may be called the heart. The primary truths are not demonstrable and yet our knowledge of them is none the less certain...Truth may be above reason and yet not contrary to reason.'[30]

There are certain basic convictions that the Christian leader must be sure of and these we shall now consider.

Concerning the Scriptures

The convictions of a leader concerning the Scriptures will affect profoundly the nature of his leadership. One who has mental reservations as to the absolute inspiration and authority of Scripture will of necessity have only a tentative note in his handling and application of divine truth. Here as elsewhere Paul sets the standard.

His only Bible was the Old Testament, and even before his conversion he treated it with reverence as the oracles of God. In his training he would commit large tracts of it to memory —an invaluable practice too little observed today. While in Japan recently a Japanese pastor told the author that he had read the Bible 86 times in the past seven years! All too many Christians have scarcely read it right through once!

In his letters Paul gives not the slightest hint that he entertained any doubts of its divine origin and inspiration. He had to face, as His Lord had done, all the same textual problems, all the alleged errors and discrepancies in the Old Testament that we have to contend with today, but there is not a scintilla of evidence that these problems ever gave him any concern. We are in good company when we take the same stand.

His confidence in the authority and integrity of Scripture is expressed in these unequivocal terms: 'All Scripture is God-breathed and is useful for teaching, rebuking, correcting and training in righteousness, so that the man of God may be thoroughly equipped for every good work' (2 Tim 3:16).

He shared his Lord's conviction that 'until heaven and earth disappear, not the smallest letter, not the least stroke of a pen, will by any means disappear from the Law until everything is accomplished' (Mt 5:18).

John Stott has said: 'The Scripture is God's Word because it is God-breathed. It originated in His mind, it issued from His mouth, although of course, it was spoken by human authors without destroying either their individuality or its divine authority in the process.'

Paul's letters teem with Old Testament references. One diligent Bible student counted 74 quotations in Romans, 29 in 1 Corinthians, 20 in 2 Corinthians, 13 in Galatians, 21 in

Ephesians, 6 in Philippians, 4 in Colossians, 7 in 1 Thessalonians, 9 in 2 Thessalonians, 2 in 1 Timothy, 4 in 2 Timothy, 3 in Titus—191 in all.

Paul was not always careful to quote the exact letter of the original, but drew out its inner spirit, as guided by the Holy Spirit; wherever he turned in the Scriptures, he discovered principles and truths that exactly fitted his own needs and those of his readers.

His unbounded confidence in the accuracy and reliability of the words of Scripture is apparent, for example, when he builds his whole argument on the use of the singular number. 'The promises were spoken to Abraham and to his seed. The Scripture does not say "and to seeds", meaning many people, but "and to your seed", meaning one person, who is Christ' (Gal 3:16). In his defence before Felix he declared: 'I believe everything that agrees with the Law, and that is written in the Prophets' (Acts 24:14).

He believed strongly in the relevance of the Old Testament Scriptures to the life and experience of New Testament Christians. Referring to the experiences of Israel in the wilderness and the judgement that fell on them for their sin, Paul wrote: 'These things happened to them as examples and were written down as warnings for us, on whom the fulfilment of the ages has come' (1 Cor 10:11). And again, 'The words "it was credited to him" (Abraham) were written not for him alone, but also for us' (Rom 4:23).

In view of Paul's obvious love and reverence for the Old Testament, and the frequent use he made of it, as R. E. Speer wrote: 'It is pathetic to think that he probably had no copy of his own. The Old Testament Scriptures were in cumbersome rolls, and they were too expensive for individuals to own. On his long journeys Paul could scarcely have carried them with him, if he had been able to purchase them.'[31] How greatly we should prize our compact, easily read and easily carried Bibles!

Concerning adverse criticism

The higher a man rises in leadership, the more he is open to the criticism and cynicism of rivals or those who oppose his views and actions. The manner in which he reacts will have far-reaching effects on his work. To play for popularity may mean forfeiting true spiritual leadership.

Paul set a valuable pattern in this regard. Though he wanted to be well thought of by his fellows, he scorned to do it at the expense of forfeiting the favour of his Lord. He expressed his ambition in 2 Corinthians 5:9: 'We make it our goal to please him', and in writing to the Galatians he asked, 'Am I now trying to win the approval of men, or of God? Or am I trying to please men? If I were still trying to please men, I would not be a servant of Christ' (Gal 1:10).

The adverse opinion of his fellows did not disturb him unduly, although he did not go out of his way to invite criticism. 'I care very little if I am judged by you, or by any human court', he wrote to the Corinthians. 'Indeed I do not even judge myself. My conscience is clear, but that does not make me innocent. It is the Lord who judges me. Therefore judge nothing before the appointed time; wait till the Lord comes' (1 Cor 4:3, 4).

Because Paul knew he was true to the 'secret things of God' that had been entrusted to him (4:1), he could afford to view mere human opinion lightly. 'I care very little if I am judged by you'. It has been pointed out that if the criticism of the Church only thirty years from Pentecost could thus be ignored by the faithful leader, the censure of the present-day tepid church need hold few terrors for us.

Nor did he fear *the world's judgement*—'any human court'. The world was not his judge, but although this was true, he was careful to preserve a balance. He also wrote: 'Do not cause anyone to stumble...even as I try to please everybody in every way. For I am not seeking my own good but the good of the many, so that they may be saved' (1 Cor 10:32,

33). He did not strain after a wooden consistency, 'that hobgoblin of small minds'.

'Mendelssohn would as soon have submitted his oratorios to the judgment of a deaf mute, or Raphael his canvas to the judgment of a man born blind', wrote D. M. Panton, 'as Paul the mysteries of God to a world that knows not God'.

He went further, and asserted that the possession of a perfectly clear conscience, invaluable though it is, did not leave him in the clear. Though conscience may flatter him, he distrusted even his own verdict on himself, for he knew the subtlety of his heart. He was not the judge. 'I do not even judge myself. My conscience is clear, but that does not make me innocent'.

'*It is the Lord who judges me*'—and He knows all the facts. He can weigh motives as well as assess facts. He is the final court of appeal. His judgement is just and infallible—*therefore* we must *suspend* judgement. 'Judge nothing before the appointed time; wait till the Lord comes'. Our powers are too limited, our knowledge so inadequate, our minds too biassed to arrive at a correct judgement. We can and must trust all to His competent hands, and in the end, 'at that time each man shall receive his praise from God'.

It remains to be said that indifference to human opinion can be disastrous if it is not linked with fear of God. But with this proviso, some independence of human assessments can be a valuable asset to the disciplined man whose aim is the glory of God. To Paul the voice of man was faint because his ear was tuned to the louder voice of God's appraisal. He did not fear man's judgement because he was conscious he stood before a higher court.

Concerning the Church

The sphere of Paul's leadership was preeminently in the Church. Indeed, from the human angle he could be said to be its chief architect. Under the guidance of the Holy Spirit he was largely responsible for fashioning it into the instrument of local fellowship and world-wide evangelism it subsequently became. He saw clearly that the Church was central in God's purposes.

While in one sense Paul was individualistic, although he was painfully conscious of the weakness and failures of the Church, he did not abandon it and set up some organization of his own, 'answerable only to God', as so frequently occurs in our day. He set out to strengthen it from within. His teaching and example give little encouragement to those who denigrate the Church.

'The individualist Christian, therefore, sitting lightly to all Church loyalties, and tempted sometimes to depreciate "organised Christianity", must expect no sympathy from Paul.'[32]

On the Damascus road he began to learn the value Christ placed on His Church. 'Saul, Saul, why do you persecute *me*' (Acts 9:4). He who touched His Church touched Christ! He learned that 'Christ loved the church and gave himself up for her' (Eph 5:25). It was God's purpose 'that now, through the church, the manifold wisdom of God should be made known to the rulers and authorities in the heavenly realms, according to his eternal purpose which he accomplished in Christ Jesus our Lord' (Eph 3:10).

This high estimate of the Church caused Paul to keep it central in thought and planning. It is interesting that most of the figures of speech Paul employs to depict the Church are not static, but vital. A living growing organism rather than a mere organization—the mystical body of Christ (Col 1:24). In the Church he saw unity amid diversity: 'Just as each of us has one body with many members, and these members do not all have the same function, so in Christ we who are many form one body, and each member belongs to all the others' (Rom 12:4,5).

Paul's concept of the marital relationship as a picture of the Church (Eph 5:25) is further developed when the

Church is called the *Bride of Christ,* with all the wealth of imagery that that figure enshrines (Rev 19:7, 9). No more tender and affectionate relationship could be imagined.

Paul did not envisage the Church as a monolithic institution, but a warm, caring family, *the family of God* with all the joyous interrelationships that true family life involves. God who 'sets the solitary in families', sets Christians in churches, where, ideally, God's people serve one another and bear one another's burdens. He is 'the Father, from whom his family in heaven and on earth derives its name (Eph 3:15).

The figure of a building, a temple which is being built with Christ as the foundation and chief cornerstone, is also adopted by Paul. It is 'a holy temple in the Lord, a dwelling in which God lives by his Spirit (Eph 2:22). Each new believer is a living stone built into that divine edifice.

The Church is also the custodian of the truth of God and the witness to it, for it is 'the church of the living God, the pillar and foundation of the truth' (1 Tim 3:15). Paul nowhere represents the Church as faultless or infallible—he knew its weaknesses too well. When he spoke of Christ presenting His Church 'as a radiant church, without stain or wrinkle or any other blemish', he knew that day was far in the future (Eph 5:27).

While the unity of the Church is to be our constant objective and concern, it must not be pursued at the expense of truth. 'Unity becomes immoral', wrote R. E. Speer, 'when it is purchased at the price of fidelity to Christ or the law of Christ in the life... Only two things were with him [Paul] ground for disruption and division. One was disloyalty and unfaithfulness to Christ, and the other, impenitent sin.'[31]

The ascended Christ enriched the Church with appropriate spiritual gifts to enable her to fulfil His eternal purpose. But even in its halcyon days some of these gifts were being abused. This gave rise to Paul's instructions in

1 Corinthians 12–14 concerning their worthy exercise. He stressed that the purpose of these gifts was for the upbuilding of the Church, not the aggrandisement of the possessor, and that the absence of genuine love would neutralize their effectiveness.

So to him the Church was the focal centre of worship and witness, of counsel and teaching, of exhortation and encouragement, of training for service.

Concerning Church discipline

One of the unwelcome responsibilities of the Christian leader is that of exercising a godly discipline. If scriptural standards and a wholesome moral and spiritual tone are to be maintained in a church or other Christian organization, it will sometimes be necessary to exercise a loving and restorative discipline. This is especially the case where doctrinal error or moral failure is involved. Throughout his letters Paul both exhorts and exemplifies the exercise of such discipline.

It is noteworthy, however, that he places special emphasis on the spirit in which the disciplining is carried out. Harsh and unloving treatment will only alienate the offender, and that is not the purpose in view. 'If anyone does not obey our instruction in this letter', Paul wrote, 'take special note of him. Do not associate with him, in order that he may feel ashamed. Yet *do not regard him as an enemy, but warn him* as a brother' (2 Thess 3:14, 15).

In the case of one who had 'caused grief', the Corinthians were exhorted to 'forgive and comfort him, so that he will not be overwhelmed by excessive sorrow. I urge you therefore to *reaffirm your love for him*' (2 Cor 2:5–8).

What should leaders do when someone is overtaken in a sin? 'You who are spiritual should *restore him gently*...or you also may be tempted (Gal 6:1). Love is an essential part of a restoring ministry. It is the person who has faced and honestly dealt with his own sins and failures who is best able to deal sympathetically and yet firmly with an offender. A spirit of meekness will achieve far more than a judgemental attitude.

Both Scripture and experience agree that in any disciplinary action, the following factors should be given full weight.

Action should be taken only after a most thorough and impartial examination of all the facts has been made.

Genuine love should be the motivation, and any action should be conducted in the most considerate manner possible.

It should be undertaken only when it is clearly for the overall good of the individual and of the work.

It should be done only with much prayer.

The paramount objective should be the spiritual help and restoration of the person concerned.

Concerning civic responsibility

In the confused and revolutionary world of today this subject is coming into more and more prominence. Many Christians are being compelled to rethink and redefine their own position in the light of prevailing conditions. Here too Paul gives a clear lead.

Living as he did in a totalitarian regime under the jurisdiction of the corrupt Felix and the monstrous Nero, Paul could have been excused if he had a rather jaundiced view of politics and civil government. Nevertheless, he strongly advocated obedience to constituted authority, be it good or bad. In writing to the Romans he gives strong reasons for his attitude: 'Everyone must submit himself to the governing authorities, for there is no authority except that which God has established. The authorities that exist have been established by God. Consequently, he who rebels against the authority is rebelling against what God has constituted, and those who do so will bring judgement on themselves. For rulers hold no terror for those who do right, but for those who do wrong' (Rom 13:1–3). He also exhorted Titus to 'remind the people to be subject to rulers and authorities, to be obedient, to be ready to do whatever is good' (Tit 3:1, 2).

The sound wisdom of this counsel took into account the fact that his fellow-countrymen in Rome were a volatile and inflammable group, whose anti-establishment activities could easily be attributed to Christians, with dire results. This was, of course, actually the case when the burning of Rome, of which Christians were entirely innocent, unleashed a fierce wave of persecution.

Although unjustly treated by the authorities on several occasions, Paul did not encourage either passive resistance or direct action. Citizens were to discharge their civil duties, pay taxes and give respect to authority: 'Give everyone what you owe him. If you owe taxes, pay taxes; if revenue, then revenue; if respect, then respect; if honour, then honour' (Rom 13:7).

More than that, Christians had a responsibility to pray for their rulers. 'I urge, then, first of all, that requests, prayers, intercession and thanksgiving be made for everyone—*for kings and all those in authority,* that we may live peaceful and quiet lives in all godliness and holiness. This is good and pleases God our Saviour' (1 Tim 2:1, 2). Whether the rulers were worthy of respect or not was irrelevant. Rather, the more unworthy they were, the greater their need of prayer.

Paul's Roman citizenship was a proud privilege, but he did not always exercise in his own interests the privileges it conferred. But where it was plainly in the best interests of his work, he did not hesitate to stand upon his rights. His experience in Philippi is a case in point. After their midnight praise session and the conversion of the jailer, 'When it was daylight, the magistrates sent their officers to the jailer with the order, "Release those men!" The jailer told Paul, "The magistrates have ordered that you and Silas be released. Now you can leave. Go in peace". But Paul said to the officers: "They beat us publicly without a trial, even though we are Roman citizens, and threw us into prison. And now do they want to get rid of us quietly? No, let them come themselves and escort us out".

'The officers reported this to the magistrates, and when they heard that Paul and Silas were Roman citizens, they were alarmed. They came to appease them and escorted them from the prison, requesting them to leave the city' (Acts 16:35–39).

In thus asserting his rights, Paul was safeguarding the future interests of the Church which was his main concern. His action made it easier for Christians in coming days. The authorities would be much more circumspect after this humiliating experience.

In a posthumous paper of Dr J. L. Nevius, he quotes approvingly these words of Dr Alexander:

'While Paul joyfully submitted to being seized, scourged, and thrown into the inner prison when all might have been avoided by a word, we cannot but admire the moral courage, calm decision and sound judgement he showed in the calm assertion of his legal rights, precisely when it was most likely to be useful to himself and others. This is enough to show how far he was from putting a fanatical or rigorous interpretation on our Saviour's principle of non-resistance (Mt 5:39) which, like many other precepts in the same discourse, teaches us what we should be willing to endure in an extreme case, but without abolishing the right and duty to determine when that case occurs.'[33]

This principle is still very applicable in missionary work where the missionary is an expatriate.

Paul was no masochist, however, and when nothing was at stake, he avoided unnecessary trouble and suffering. 'As they stretched him out to flog him, Paul said to the centurion standing there, "Is it legal for you to flog a Roman citizen who hasn't been found guilty?"'. There were times however, when he submitted to flogging (e.g. 2 Cor 11:24), but in this case he judged his suffering would achieve no good purpose.

Later, he availed himself of his right to appeal to Caesar, a choice that had far-reaching influence on the future course of the Church (Acts 25:8–12). He made his appeal because he saw 'that the time had come to determine the status of Christianity before the Roman law'.

Concerning conscience

'I strive always to keep my conscience clear before God and man' (Acts 24:16).

A condemning conscience is no asset to a leader. More than any other New Testament writer, Paul gives clear teaching on the function of conscience—a very important aspect of truth, since conscience contributes so much to our emotional well-being. Ignorance of its function or persistent disobedience to its dictum can lead to serious spiritual disorders. It is therefore necessary for the leader or counsellor to know what Scripture has to say on the subject. Paul's frequent reference to the state of his conscience shows how important he regarded its proper functioning.

Conscience has been defined as the testimony and judgement of the soul which gives approval or disapproval to the acts of the will. It seems to be a special activity of the intellect and emotions which enables one to distinguish between good and evil—to perceive moral distinctions.

It is this faculty which renders man's sin culpable and distinguishes him from animals. The word signifies 'knowledge held in conjunction with another'—in this instance, God. It thus carries the idea of man being co-witness with God for or against himself, according to his own estimate of his actions.

Conscience, however, is not an executive faculty. It has no power to make men do right or cease doing wrong. It delivers its verdict, produces the appropriate emotion, but leaves it to the will of man to act in the light of its judgement. It has no further responsibility. It is like a thermometer which, though detecting and indicating the temperature, never creates or modifies that temperature. When we obey our conscience, as someone has said, we live in the beatitudes. When we disobey, like John the Baptist, it cries—'It is not lawful!'

A condemning conscience

Paul lists four progressive states of a conscience that condemns.

A weak conscience that is morbid and overscrupulous. Paul illustrates this from the case of food offered to idols. 'Some people are still so accustomed to idols that when they eat such food they think of it as having been sacrificed to an idol, and since their conscience is weak, it is defiled …When you sin against your brothers in this way and wound their weak conscience, you sin against Christ' (1 Cor 8:7, 12).

This person's conscience reacts faithfully according to its light, but like a compass with a weak magnetic current, it tends to vacillate. The result is that its possessor is constantly tormented with doubt as to the propriety of an action, and digs up in unbelief what has been sown in faith. There can be two reasons for such weakness—imperfect knowledge of God's Word and will, with a consequent imperfect faith; or an unsurrendered will that gives a vacillating choice. The corrective is to face the issues involved clearly in the light of Scripture, come to a decision according to one's best judgement and resolutely leave it there.

A weak conscience easily degenerates into a defiled conscience (1 Cor 8:7). If we persist in some action against

which conscience has protested, we thereby defile it and
prevent its faithful functioning, just as dust clogs the delicate
mechanism of a watch and causes it to record the wrong
time. This is especially true in the realm of moral purity.
'To the pure, all things are pure, but to those who are
corrupted...nothing is pure. In fact, both their minds and
consciences are corrupted' (Tit 1:15).

A *disregarded conscience may become habitually evil and
guilty*, coming to regard good as evil, and evil as good.
'Having our hearts sprinkled to cleanse us from a guilty
conscience' (Heb 10:22). If its possessor is determined to
do evil, its protesting voice will grow increasingly faint.

Habitual defiance of conscience reduces it to complete
insensitivity, and it ceases to function. 'Such teachings
come through hypocritical liars, *whose consciences have
been seared as with a hot iron*' (1 Tim 4:2). When conscience
becomes cauterized, it no longer protests, and no appeal
succeeds.

Failure to heed the voice of conscience leads to serious
consequences, Paul warns. 'Holding on to faith and a good
conscience. Some have rejected these and so have ship-
wrecked their faith' (1 Tim 1:19).

A commending conscience

Here too, Paul lists four progressive states. An approving
conscience is a prize beyond rubies. Conscience is just as
faithful in commending the right as in condemning the
wrong. 'If our hearts [consciences] do not condemn us, we
have confidence before God' (1 Jn 3:21). Paul lists four
desirable states of conscience.

A *clear conscience*. 'They must keep hold of the deep
truths of the faith with *a clear conscience*' (1 Tim 3:9).
'I thank God whom I serve...with a clear conscience'
(2 Tim 1:3). A clear or pure conscience is acutely sensitive
to the approach of evil. It is kept pure and clean as we fully

obey the light shed on our conduct by the Word of God.

A good conscience is the possession of one who accepts the dictates of his clear conscience in all things. 'The goal of this command is love, which comes from a pure heart and a good conscience' (1 Tim 1:5). 'Holding on to faith and a good conscience' (1 Tim 1:19). Its reproof is welcomed and obeyed.

A conscience void of offence. 'Herein do I exercise myself, to have always a conscience void of offence toward God, and toward men' (Acts 24:16 KJV). This is the happy state in which no accusing voice shatters peace with God, or mars relationships with men. To forfeit this serenity and heart-rest for the sake of some brief gratification is to pay too high a price.

A perfected conscience, through the cleansing of the blood of Christ. 'Gifts and sacrifices... offered were not able to clear the conscience of the worshipper' (Heb 9:9). 'How much more, then, will the blood of Christ... cleanse our consciences' (Heb 9:14).

Conscience has no cure for its own ills; so the provision made in the blood of Christ must be personally appropriated if its owner is to enjoy peace with God.

It remains to be said that conscience is not infallible, but is a fluctuating factor which reacts faithfully to its accepted standards. The conscience of a Hindu, which in former times would protest loudly against the killing of a cow, would offer no protest when a widow was burned on the funeral pyre. It is a matter of the standard to which conscience bears witness. The consciences of those who conducted the Inquisition inwardly approved their actions, but that did not justify them.

The delicate mechanism of conscience was thrown off balance at the fall. Every conscience requires adjustment, and will function aright only when it is adjusted to the standards of Scripture. Paul asserted that this required strenuous moral effort on his part. 'So I strive to keep my conscience clear'.

Paul himself, blinded by prejudice and bigotry, had reacted to a conscience that was not adjusted to Scripture, and how bitterly he repented when he saw the true nature of the actions which his conscience had previously approved.

The person who is troubled by a condemning conscience should remember that *upon repentance*, the worst sin can be forgiven, and will pass immediately and completely from the conscience. The Holy Spirit, who delights to apply the solvent of the blood of Christ to the defiled conscience in response to faith, also delights to enable the believer to walk with a conscience void of offence.

Concerning the devil

The person in a position of leadership who ignores the activities of our unseen adversary, the devil, has obviously not seriously studied the teachings of our Lord or of Paul on this subject. There is a Chinese proverb that runs: 'Know your enemy; then in one hundred battles you will be victorious one hundred times'. No leader can afford to be a spiritual ignoramus on this subject.

The classic passage on the spiritual warfare of the believer with Satan and the powers of darkness—Ephesians 6:10–18 —comes from the pen of the Apostle. Sagacious leader that he was, he was alert to the necessity of instructing his followers concerning the foes they would meet, and the character of the warfare in which they would inevitably be engaged and the way of victory. To him the devil was no figment of an overheated imagination, but a wily and experienced antagonist. He was too wise to underestimate the calibre of his opponent. He would have approved Victor Hugo's contention that a good general must penetrate the brain of his enemy.

That Paul had done this, and was therefore 'not ignorant of his devices', the following verses demonstrate:

Satan himself masquerades as an angel of light (2 Cor 11:14).

You followed the ways of the ... ruler of the kingdom of the air, the spirit who is now at work in those who are disobedient (Eph 2:2).

The coming of the lawless one will be in accordance with the work of Satan displayed in all kinds of counterfeit miracles, signs and wonders (2 Thess 2:9).

The god of this age has blinded the minds of unbelievers (2 Cor 4:4).

I am sending you to ... turn them from ... the power of Satan to God (Acts 26:18).

It was the Apostle's consistent teaching that in his walk and witness the Christian would meet with the implacable hatred and opposition of both the world and the devil and those evil spirits who have allied themselves with him. 'Our struggle is not against flesh and blood, but against the rulers, against the authorities, against the powers of this dark world and against the spiritual forces of evil in the heavenly realms' (Eph 6:12). He believed that unseen forces rule the world, and that these supernatural powers could be vanquished only by the use of supernatural weapons and he employed them. He proved a wise and doughty leader in this spiritual warfare.

Although Satan's power is limited, not inherent but delegated, he is more than a match for the strongest Christian. Paul acknowledged that he has been granted some measure of control as 'the ruler of the kingdom of the air'. He also indicated that in this warfare there can be no such thing as a pacifist. True the warfare is spiritual, but it is desperately real. It is a struggle, a wrestling. Our foes will contest God's eternal purpose at every point, and He is counting on our cooperation. At this late day in world history, we are seeing a fulfilment of Revelation 12:12: 'But woe to the earth and the sea, because the devil has gone down to you! He is filled with fury, because he knows that his time is short.' He knows that the victory of Christ spells the end of his dominion, and is resisting desperately in an attempt to stave off final defeat.

God's strategy is for the believer to stand fast and hold his ground in the position of privilege and security in which He has placed us. 'God raised us up with Christ and seated us with him in the heavenly realms in Christ Jesus' (Eph 2:6). Our responsibility is to 'stand...stand...stand' (Eph 6:11, 13, 14).

Satan's plan is to dislodge the Christian from this position, and drive him to lower levels, forgetful of his privileged position in 'the heavenlies'. He tries to induce him to make war with carnal weapons; but Paul warns that we do not wage this war as the world does. 'The weapons we fight with are not the weapons of the world. On the contrary, they have divine power to demolish strongholds' (2 Cor 10:4). A bayonet would be a poor weapon against a hydrogen bomb! The fact that it is a spiritual war determines the character of the weapons.

Chained to a soldier as he frequently was, Paul would be very conscious of the nature and purpose of his armour. He was deeply concerned that his followers should not enter the battle defenceless. So he takes up this figure and counsels the Ephesian Christians—and us—to appropriate the divine power and strengthening He has graciously provided: 'Be strong in the Lord and in his mighty power' (Eph 6:10). Also, the Christian warrior must don 'the full armour of God'—provided by God. To omit putting on one piece would leave an Achilles' heel exposed.

Because the devil was a liar from the beginning, the combatant must buckle *the belt of truth* (v. 14) around his waist. As the soldier's belt encompassed his waist and held all the other pieces of armour in place, so the truth of God is to encompass and unify the whole life. This leaves no room for hypocrisy or insincerity.

The function of the breastplate was to protect the vital organs, so he must *'put on the breastplate of righteousness'* (v. 14). Christ is our righteousness (1 Cor 1:30), but the fighter too must be actually righteous in life. He is to wear integrity as a coat of mail.

In warfare it is important that the soldier be well shod or he will be unable to stand his ground. He is to have 'feet shod with the equipment of the gospel of peace' (v. 15 RSV). He must be swift and ready to run with the Good News—the antithesis of lethargy and ease.

The whole length of the body was covered by a large oblong leather shield which was saturated in water before battle. The soldier must hold this in place. 'In addition to all this, take up *the shield of faith*, with which you can extinguish all the flaming arrows of the evil one' (v. 16). The enemy's arrows, tipped with flaming pitch, would be extinguished when they struck the water-soaked leather. Satan's arrows can take the form of irrational fears, or sudden and unexpected attacks, especially in the realm of the mind. The exercise of a living, confident faith in our victorious Saviour and the intelligent use of the Word of God will effectually quench the flames of temptation.

'The helmet of salvation' (v. 17) is the last piece of defensive armour, and it of course protects the head. An unprotected mind is a ready prey to Satan's seductions. If we allow it to lie fallow and little cultivated, we are inviting the enemy to sow weeds. It is the mind that Satan seeks to control, because it directs all else. The tragic condition of the world today is mute testimony to the success of his endeavours. The helmet has to do with our hope. 'Putting on faith and love as a breastplate, and the hope of salvation as a helmet', the Apostle says elsewhere (1 Thess 5:8). Christ's salvation brings us hope in a hopeless world. We can be as sure as God that there is victory for us (1 Cor 15:57).

'*The sword of the Spirit,* which is the word of God' (v. 17) is for both defence and attack. It was the only weapon our Lord employed in his epochal conflict with the devil in the wilderness. It proved mightily effective because He knew how to wield it expertly. It is the soldier's responsibility to master the Word of God so thoroughly, so to store his mind with it, that the Holy Spirit can call to his memory the appropriate truth as a conquering weapon in the moment of need.

There is a self-evident connection between the sword of the spirit and the weapon of 'all prayer' (v. 18). The battle for the minds and souls of men is fought and won primarily in the place of prayer. We are to wage war with 'all forms of prayer', and in addition it must be 'all-out prayer', for this is total war in which there is no truce.

So then, the purpose of the 'full armour of God' is to enable us to stand our ground in the evil day, and having done all, to stand victorious over all our foes.

> Soldiers of Christ arise
> And put your armour on,
> Strong in the strength which God supplies
> Through His eternal Son.
>
> Stand then in His great might
> With all His strength endued;
> And take to arm you for the fight
> The panoply of God.
>
> Leave no unguarded place,
> No weakness of the soul,
> Take every virtue, every grace
> And fortify the whole.
>
> *Charles Wesley*

Concerning doubtful things

All of us, and leaders especially, at times have to decide whether a certain course is right or wrong. Sometimes the problem is not our own, but as leaders we are asked to counsel and guide others in this area. Paul's writings provide us with helpful guidelines.

Some interpret Paul's statement: 'We are not under law but under grace' (Rom 6:15) as meaning that under the benificent reign of grace there is no place for the prohibitions and taboos of the Mosaic law. But this is far from being the case. It is Paul's clear teaching that we are not 'under the law' *as a means of our justification*, but that does not mean that we can become lawless, for 'we are under law to Christ', bound by new but no less powerful bonds.

It is a striking fact that every one of the commandments in the decalogue except, significantly enough, the law concerning the sabbath, is not only repeated in the New Testament, but its scope is greatly widened. For example, our Lord said: 'You have heard that it was said, "Do not commit adultery." But I tell you that anyone who looks at a woman lustfully has already committed adultery with her in his heart' (Mt 5:27–28).

We are now under law to Christ, bound by the bonds of love as a new way of life. The genius of the New Covenant lies in the fact that rather than enacting a new set of rules and regulations, it enunciates principles which, if we apply them correctly, cover every case. The inexorable demands, 'Thou shalt...thou shalt not', are replaced by gracious divine undertakings, 'I will...I will' (Heb 8:10–12).

Many vexed questions may be disposed of almost automatically by asking and answering the following questions:

Is it beneficial and helpful?

'Everything is permissible', Paul writes, 'but not everything is beneficial' (1 Cor 10:23). If I take this course, will it make me a better and more mature Christian? Will it make my life more profitable to God and to my fellow-man?

Is it constructive?

Does it edify and build up the Church? 'Everything is permissible, but not everything is constructive' (1 Cor 10:23). Although things may be legitimate, they are not all of equal value. I should therefore ask myself, 'Will this course tend to build up my Christian character? Will it equip me for the task of building up the Church?

Will it tend to enslave me?

'Everything is permissible for me—but I will not be mastered by anything', Paul declared (1 Cor 6:12). Even things lawful in themselves can exercise an undue influence on us, occupy too much of our time, and thus hold us back from God's best for us. An undue amount of secular reading, or an excessive amount of TV viewing, for example, can dull our appetite for the Word of God. We have to choose our priorities carefully, even in the area of lawful things.

Will it strengthen me against temptation?

There is no use praying, 'Lead us not into temptation', if we voluntarily walk into it. Anything that tends to make sin less sinful or easier to commit must be abjured.

This does not apply merely to things that are lewd or vulgar. Some things may be intellectual and beautiful, but if our pursuit of them dims our spiritual vision, or hinders our running the race, they are weights which should be laid aside. 'Let us throw off everything that hinders' (Heb 12:1).

Though differing in setting, the problems confronting the Christians in Rome do not differ essentially from those we face today. Paul's counsel in these areas is strangely contemporary, and if we accept and act on the principles he enunciates it will lead us into a new and joyous liberty.

Liberty of judgement on doubtful things

'One man's faith allows him to eat everything, but another man, whose faith is weak, eats only vegetables. The man who eats everything must not look down on him who does not, and the man who does not eat everything must not condemn the man who does, for God has accepted him' (Rom 14:2, 3). The problem under discussion had its origin in food offered to idols. Paul points out that to a well-taught Christian an idol is nothing, and he feels free to eat food that had been offered to it. But to another who is weak in the faith, it is a stumbling-block.

As no vital doctrine was at stake, he urged tolerance in this potential cause of friction. Within the Church, in matters which are not clearly erroneous or are purely cultural, there is room for genuine differences of opinion, and we are to uphold the right of our brother to entertain opinions contrary to our own.

The right of personal conviction

'One man considers one day more sacred than another; another man considers every day alike. Each one should be fully convinced in his own mind' (Rom 14:5). It is easy to be like the chameleon and change our theological colour to suit our company. It is easy to be swayed by theological preference or prejudice rather than the clear teaching of Scripture. Paul says we must come to clear convictions of our own that are squarely based on Scripture, and not allow our decisions or conduct to be dictated by someone else. We have to live with the outcome of our decisions, so we should have our own convictions.

Accountability to God alone

'Who are you to judge someone else's servant? To his own master he stands or falls...So then, each of us will give an account of himself to God' (Rom 14:4, 12). We are all members of society and have responsibility towards it, but we are finally answerable to God alone. One is our Master, and no one can arrogate to himself His sovereign rights over us. The certainty that the judgement seat lies ahead for every believer should deeply influence his conduct.

'You, then, why do you judge your brother?' Paul asks. 'Or why do you look down on your brother? For we will all stand before God's judgment seat' (Rom 14:10)

Absence of censoriousness

It is not our prerogative to criticize or judge our brother's actions, that right belongs to God alone. 'Therefore, let us stop passing judgment on one another. Instead, make up your mind not to put any stumbling-block or obstacle in your brother's way' (Rom 14:13). In the last day we will be judged by God, not by one another. We should always credit others with the same degree of sincerity as we would expect them to accord to us.

Abstinence in the interests of others

We are not to live for our own pleasure alone, or to be absorbed solely in our own interests. We must take into account the possible effects of our lives on others. Accordingly 'it is better not to eat meat or drink wine or to do anything that will cause your brother to fall' (Rom 14:21).

The freedom some Christians claim for social or moderate drinking has often proved the downfall of the weaker brother who does not have the same strength of will. It is for us voluntarily to limit our own legitimate enjoyment, in the interests of the weaker brother. 'We who are strong ought to bear with the failings of the weak and not to please ourselves' (Rom 15:1).

Abstinence from things of doubtful legitimacy

The very fact that we have doubts raises the presumption that the matter under review is questionable. All our actions should carry the positive assurance of faith.

'Blessed is the man who does not condemn himself by what he approves. But the man who has doubts is condemned if he eats, because his eating is not from faith; and everything that does not come from faith is sin' (Rom 14:22, 23). The presence of continuing doubt should be regarded as a call to delay action until clearer light emerges. Through prayer and study of the relevant Scriptures, the Holy Spirit will either remove the doubt, or give the conviction that this is not the will of God.

On the other hand, our problem might be that we have a weak or uninstructed conscience that needs education by the Word of God. It is very possible that as a result of our background and past associations, or because of tradition or prejudice, we may have doubts about things the Bible does not condemn. In such matters we should depend on the gracious ministry of the Holy Spirit to 'lead us into all truth'.

Concerning finance

The only authentic saying of our Lord, outside the four Gospels, has been preserved for us by Paul—'The Lord Jesus himself said, "It is more blessed to give than to receive"' (Acts 20:35). It can be said with certainty that Paul himself qualified for the beatitude he commended.

In no area did he exercise more meticulous care than in the sensitive area of finance. In this, he sets an important example for the Christian leader. It would hardly be an exaggeration to say that more leaders have lost spiritual power through a wrong use or a wrong attitude toward money than through any other single cause.

Our Lord accorded an astonishing prominence to money in His teaching. It figured in some way in one verse out of six in the Synoptic Gospels, and in sixteen of His thirty-eight parables. He thus recognized that money is one of the central realities of life from the cradle to the grave. It is one of the dominating topics of conversation, and one of the most absorbing objects of pursuit. Money is a subject concerning which one cannot be neutral.

Paul was very conscious of this ubiquitous problem, and was therefore scrupulous in his financial dealings and stewardship. So as to ease the burden of his support from the young churches, he earned his own living, and at times supported his colleagues as well. He was 'financially clean', and set a noble example of generosity.

Paul states his financial philosophy in 1 Timothy 6:5–10 where he refers to 'men of corrupt mind, who have been robbed of the truth and who think that godliness is a means to financial gain. But godliness with contentment is great gain. For we brought nothing into the world, and we can take nothing out of it. But if we have food and clothing, we will be content with that. People who want to get rich fall into a trap and into many foolish and harmful desires that plunge men into ruin and destruction. For the love of money is a root of all kinds of evil. Some people, eager for money, have wandered from the faith and pierced themselves with many griefs.'

This is, alas, the story of too many Christians, including leaders. So Paul warns the young pastor as he was about to undertake his new assignment.

He was careful not to assume too much personal responsibility in financial matters. When the Corinthian Christians collected money for their needy friends in Jerusalem, he would not assume the responsibility of taking the gift. He felt that the donors should be the ones to take it to the recipients, and he would thus be clear of any suspicion of financial dishonesty.

Systematic and proportionate giving was encouraged by the Apostle. 'On the first day of every week', Paul counselled the Corinthians, 'each one of you should set aside a sum of money in keeping with his income, saving it up, so that when I come no collections will have to be made. Then, when I arrive, I will give letters of introduction to the men you approve and send them with your gift to Jerusalem. If it seems advisable for me to go also, they will accompany me' (1 Cor 16:2–4)

This procedure showed true wisdom, for in new and developing churches in areas where the standard of living is low, the stewardship of money collected often proves a tremendous temptation to the one responsible. For this reason it is always wise for more than one person to be involved in the counting and stewardship of money.

In stimulating the Corinthian church to greater generosity, Paul cited the generosity of the One 'who for our sakes became poor', and also the lavish liberality of the poor Macedonian church: 'Out of the most severe trial, their overflowing joy and their extreme poverty welled up in rich generosity. For I testify that they gave as much as they were able, and even beyond their ability. Entirely on their own, they urgently pleaded with us for the privilege of sharing in this service to the saints' (2 Cor 8:2–5). Here is a new type of fund-raising, in which the donor begs for the opportunity to give to the cause! The Macedonians demonstrated that it was more blessed to give than to receive.

Concerning guidance

There is no area in which a leader requires greater spiritual wisdom than in that of guidance—discerning the will and leading of God in any situation. Those who have not found themselves in positions of major leadership may well imagine that greater experience and a longer walk with God would result in much greater ease in discerning the will of God in perplexing situations. This is by no means always the case. The divine method is, more often, to treat the leader as a mature adult, to leave more and more to his spiritual judgement, and give fewer tangible evidences of

His guidance than in earlier years. Perplexity in obtaining clear direction can add to the inevitable pressures incidental to any responsible office. Paul's experience affords some helpful lessons in guidance.

Though he had responded immediately to the call of God on the Damascus road, his career as a missionary did not commence until he had been working for a period with the church at Antioch, ten or eleven years later.

While the multi-racial leaders of that church were 'worshipping the Lord and fasting, the Holy Spirit said, "Set apart for me Barnabas and Saul for the work to which I have called them"' (Acts 13:2). This divine summons marked the real beginning of Paul's missionary career. To his ardent spirit those previous years of preparation must have dragged by on leaden feet. At last he is to be set free and sent forth on his world mission.

He did not embark on his missionary career until his personal call—'I *have* called them'—was confirmed *to* the local church with which he was associated, and then confirmed *by* them. 'So after they had fasted and prayed, they placed their hands upon them and sent them off' (Acts 13:3). Thus the *corporate* guidance of the church leaders confirmed Paul's *personal* guidance. The Antioch church established a precedent that could well be a model for churches today. It means a great deal to both church and missionary if the individual call of the latter is ratified by the leaders of the church with which he is identified.

It is significant that Paul, superbly trained though he was, served for a period with a more experienced worker from the church which sent him out, and that, not only during his first term of missionary service but also through part of the second. But what a senior missionary he was privileged to serve under! Barnabas, the son of encouragement or consolation! Without doubt this godly, large-hearted man, exercised a great influence on Paul during these training days. And it says a great deal for Barnabas that when his junior streaked ahead of him and assumed leadership of the team, as was inevitable sooner or later, there was not a trace of resentment or jealousy.

One of the most helpful scripture passages illustrating God's method of guidance is Acts 16:6–10. In interpreting this passage it is important to bear in mind that the call from Macedonia is not to be regarded as on all fours with an *initial missionary call,* but rather indicates the divine method of redirecting one who has already responded to the initial call into a specific sphere of work. It was the Holy Spirit who chose the time and place of service for Paul and his colleagues.

From this passage we learn that God guides at times by inward monitions or prohibitions. 'Paul and his companions travelled throughout the regions of Phrygia and Galatia, having been kept by the Holy Spirit from preaching the word in the province of Asia. When they came to the border of Mysia, they tried to enter Bithynia, but the Spirit of Jesus would not allow them to. So they passed by Mysia and went down to Troas' (vv. 6–8).

Asia and Bithynia were to hear the word later, but at this time the divine strategy was that the Good News should travel westward. The winds of the Spirit were blowing in Europe, which was now ripe for harvest. Paul and his band were to be privileged to put in the sickle.

Spiritually sensitive, Paul responded to the restraint of the Spirit, and did not press forward in self-will. Instead he drew aside to Troas, to discover in prayer and consultation with his companions the geographical will of God for them. The tiny band little realized the world-shaking consequences that hung on their decision! The issue before them was clear—either go back home, or push forward and cross the sea. How could they know which was God's will? God did not leave them long in doubt. The negative guidance of closed doors was followed by positive direction.

'During the night Paul had a vision of a man of Macedonia

standing and begging him, "Come over to Macedonia and help us"' (v. 9). Note that the vision came to Paul *after* he had gone forward in obedience to the Great Commission, and it formed only one element in his guidance. He had already completed his first assignment, and was now reaching out to what lay beyond.

Even after the vision, Paul as leader was careful to check his guidance with his colleagues, and to involve them in any decision. In the event, they were brought to a Spirit-wrought unity of mind. 'After Paul had seen the vision, we got ready at once to leave for Macedonia, concluding that God had called us to preach the gospel to them' (v. 10). A. T. Robertson sees in this mutual consultation 'a good illustration of the proper use of reason in connection with revelation, to decide whether it is a revelation of God, to find out what it means for us and see that we obey the revelation.'[34]

Thus, before taking a further step, Paul assured himself that his vision was in line with the word of God, was witnessed to by the Holy Spirit, was agreeable to his companions and was approved by his own judgement. This double-checking of his guidance saved him from dismay when he met a hostile reception and they found themselves with bleeding backs in the jail at Philippi. Instead of doubting the validity of their guidance when things seemed to go wrong, they turned to prayer and praise. How could the devil defeat men like that?

Concerning rights

One factor that contributed to Paul's massive stature and coloured his leadership was his attitude to his rights. In a day when far greater emphasis is laid on claiming one's rights than on fulfilling one's obligations, Paul's attitude administers a wholesome contemporary corrective. The leader must be very sensitive in this area if he is to exercise a growing influence.

In 1 Corinthians 9, a chapter which gives in part the secret of Paul's soul-winning ministry, he seven times refers to his rights in the gospel. This piece of autobiography carries a powerful message for the person whose ambition it is to become an effective soul-winner and leader.

Few would challenge the contention that if he is to become such, he must achieve victory over the *wrong* things in his life. But not every Christian worker recognizes that the renunciation of things that in themselves are *right* may be involved. In this, Paul set a shining example. Referring to his right to church support, he claimed, 'we put up with anything rather than hinder the gospel of Christ' (9:12). It is the small man who is always asserting his rights.

Paul recognized that although certain things may be legitimate in themselves, they may well limit his ministry. As we have seen, he had just written, 'Everything is permissible for me, but everything is not beneficial'. 'Everything is permissible for me—but I will not be mastered by anything' (6:12). Later he would write, 'Everything is permissible—but not everything is constructive' (10:23). He knew it was very possible to indulge legitimate tastes and appetites to an inordinate degree, and thus become enslaved. There must be victory in the realm of legitimate desire as well as in that of illegitimate indulgence.

Oswald Chambers maintained in his trenchant style, 'If we are willing to give up only *wrong* things for Jesus, let us never talk about being in love with Him. Anyone will give up wrong things if he knows how. But are we prepared to give up the best we have for Jesus Christ? The only right a Christian has is the right to give up his rights'.

To be the best for God some voluntary renunciations are necessary (Lk 14:33). If we wish to scale the heights for God, we must face up to this challenge of voluntary renunciation.

Our example in this, as in everything else, is our Lord Himself. As 'heir of all things' He enjoyed and exercised rights beyond our wildest imaginations. And yet for our sakes he renounced them one by one. The renunciation of rights began when He rose from His eternal throne and

> forsook the courts of everlasting day,
> and chose with us a darksome house of mortal clay.

> *John Milton*

The greatest sacrifice is that of those who have the most to surrender. Christ forsook the congenial company of angels for the hostility of men; the comforts of home for an itinerant life; the riches of heaven for the penury of earth. At last, in love He renounced even His place in humanity and suffered the pangs of death as a criminal.

If sacrifice is indeed 'the ecstasy of giving the best we have to the one we love the most', it inevitably follows that there will often be lower rights that must be renounced for love of Him.

If I pay my fare on a bus, I have an inalienable right to a seat if there is one available. But when a tired mother with a baby in one arm and parcels in the other enters a crowded bus, although no one can challenge my right to my seat, I have the higher right to waive that right and offer my seat to the lady. And shall we do less for our Lord?

In this chapter (1 Cor 9) Paul asserts his rights in four realms—

The right to gratify normal appetite (v. 4)

The right to normal marital life (v. 5)

The right to normal rest and recreation (v. 6)

The right to adequate remuneration (v. 12)

To Paul, the joy and obligation of sharing the gospel was vastly more important than gratifying his appetite or indulging his desire for leisure. He was no ascetic but was determined that he would not be dominated by his body.

'I will not be bossed by appetite,' said John Wesley. So for two years he lived on a diet of—potatoes! It was this inflexible purpose to be the best for God that gave Wesley such a tremendous influence on his own generation. 'We have not made use of this right', Paul claimed (v. 12).

For love of Christ and in the interests of soul-winning effectiveness Paul forewent the exercise of his right to be accompanied by a wife. 'Not making full use of my right in the gospel' (v. 18), was his characteristic attitude. He did not squeeze the last drop out of his rights.

He strongly asserted his right to be supported by those to whom he ministered. 'The Lord has commanded that those who preach the gospel should receive their living from the gospel' (v. 14). 'But I have not used any of these rights' (v. 15). He feared lest he should be lumped with the greedy priesthood, and he also desired to maintain independence in the exercise of his apostolic authority. So he elected to support himself by his tent-making. However, on some occasions he accepted gifts from churches.

It takes uncommonly strong motivation to induce a leader or anyone else to adopt this attitude to his rights. 'Though I am free, and belong to no man', wrote Paul, 'I make myself a slave to everyone, to win as many as possible' (v. 19). And a slave has no rights!

A missionary in China shared his experience. 'When I came to China, I was all ready to *eat bitterness* [Chinese idiom for "suffering hardship"] and like it. That hasn't troubled me particularly. It takes a little time to get your palate and your digestion used to Chinese food, of course, but that was no harder than I expected. Another thing, however'—and he paused significantly—'*another thing* that I had never thought about came up to make trouble. I had to *eat loss!* Chinese idiom for "suffering the infringement of one's rights". I found that I couldn't stand up for my rights—that I couldn't even *have* any rights. I found that I had to give them up, every one, and that was the hardest thing of all' (12). In the words of Jesus, he had to 'deny himself', and that is never easy.

Concerning slavery

The charge has been levelled against Paul that he should have given a stronger lead against the ghastly slave traffic. But the charge will not stick. He is blamed for appearing to accept the slavery of Onesimus without protest, instead of telling Philemon the slave-owner that it was inconsistent with Christian principles. But if we sincerely endeavour to put ourselves in Paul's situation, we will more readily understand the reason why he did not assume the role of a revolutionary crusader.

When Paul said to Philemon that Onesimus was to be to him 'no longer as a slave but better than a slave, a dear brother' (Philem v. 16)—both in the flesh and in the Lord—then he laid a foundation for a new order that was bound to come.[35] As some put it, he did not cut the tree down, but he ring-barked it.

Gibbon, the historian, gave it as his opinion that in AD 57 one half of the population of the Roman Empire were slaves. The question of the status of slaves was therefore a most important social issue in the life of the Church of that day, and the manner in which Paul handled it has lessons for leaders of today.

In the culture of those days a slave was not a person, only a chattel. His status was no higher than that of an animal. Current literature portrayed the inhuman cruelty with which many slaves were treated. There were many, however, who received very humane treatment.

One could well have imagined that a firebrand like Paul would at once have sprung into the arena, set up a strong anti-slavery movement and inflamed the slaves against their masters. The manner in which he handled this hot issue has caused some, both now and in the past, to conclude that he approved slavery and was rather insensitive to social injustice. This was far from being the case. Guided by the Holy Spirit, he adopted a method which in the prevailing conditions, was best calculated to achieve the amelioration of the lot of the slave.

His counsel to Timothy was eminently wise in the circumstances he faced. A social revolution on so vast a scale as would be necessary could not be achieved overnight. Any attempt to do so would have brought untold persecution to the Christians. So Paul advised Timothy: 'All who are under the yoke of slavery should consider their masters worthy of full respect, so that God's name and our teaching may not be slandered' (1 Tim 6:1).

Insubordination was out of order for the Christian slave. Instead he was to be content with his lot. 'Were you a slave when you were called? Don't let it trouble you—although if you can gain your freedom, do so. For he who was a slave when he was called is the Lord's freedman; similarly, he who was a free man when he was called is Christ's slave' (1 Cor 7:21, 22). He thus calls on the Christian slave to rejoice in the spiritual blessing and freedom which faith in Christ had brought to him.

It is interesting to note that Paul warned against an impertinent or undue familiarity of slaves towards their Christian masters, as could very well have been the case. 'Those who have believing masters are not to show less respect for them because they are brothers. Instead, they are to serve them even better, because those who benefit from their service are believers, and dear to them' (1 Tim 6:2).

He told Titus to 'teach slaves to be subject to their masters in everything, to try to please them... and not to steal from them, but to show that they can be fully trusted, so that in every way they will make the teaching about God our Saviour attractive' (Tit 2:9, 10).

The duty of the master to the slave is not left unstressed. 'Masters, treat your slaves in the same way. Do not threaten them, since you know that he who is both their Master and yours is in heaven, and there is no favouritism with him' (Eph 6:9).

It was in the Church that the liberation of the slaves began. Within the Church Paul enunciated and enforced principles that, acted upon, would strike off their shackles. He taught equality in Christ. 'There is neither Jew nor Greek, slave nor free, male nor female, for you are all one in Christ' (Gal 3:28). Brotherly love must characterize all their relationships. 'Be devoted one to another in brotherly love' (Rom 12:10). Both masters and slaves must respect their mutual rights and perform their mutual duties (Eph 6:5–9).

As the Church grew in number and these principles were increasingly practised, the seeds of social reform began to germinate, and gradually enlightenment came. Under Christian emperors slavery began to dwindle. The process was slow, but wherever Christianity has come, slavery has gone. Christianity and slavery can never live together in peaceful coexistence.

Concerning suffering

The leader must have his own philosophy of the problem of suffering, as he will frequently be called upon to counsel his followers who find themselves faced with suffering. Paul could urge his young colleague, 'Take your share of suffering', because he himself was prepared to do the same, and set the example.

Alexander the Great's veterans threatened mutiny on the grounds that he was indifferent to their hardship and their wounds. He sprang up on the dais and said to the disgruntled men: 'Come, now, who of you have wounds, let him bare himself and I will show mine. No member of my body is without its wounds. I have been wounded by the sword, by the arrow from the bow, by the missile from the catapult. I have been pelted with stones and pounded with clubs while leading you to victory and glory.'[36]

Paul, a greater conqueror than Alexander the Great,

could say that too. 'Finally, let no one cause me trouble', he challenged his opponents, 'for I bear on my body the marks of Jesus' (Gal 6:17).

More than any other apostle Paul was exposed to suffering, hardship and distress. The catalogue of his trials he reluctantly gives in 2 Corinthians 11:23–28 seems more than any human being could survive. And yet he emerged triumphant, more than conqueror.

More than any other apostle, too, Paul had been granted special revelations by the Lord. Referring to one such incident he wrote, 'Although there is nothing to be gained, I will go on to visions and revelations from the Lord. I know a man in Christ who fourteen years ago was caught up to the third heaven... and I know that this man... was caught up to Paradise. He heard inexpressible things, things that man is not permitted to tell' (2 Cor 12:1–4).

These were no ordinary experiences. Indeed, they were so unique that they presented Paul with a great temptation to pride. God was deeply concerned lest he succumb to this temptation and thus limit his ministry. So He introduced an equalizing factor—'To keep me from being conceited because of these surpassingly great revelations, there was given me a thorn in my flesh, a messenger of Satan, to torment me' (12:7).

Paul was strangely reticent about the exact nature of the thorn. Concerning this, opinion is sharply divided. Some have thought it was *mental or spiritual*—sensual desires, depression, doubt. Others, that it was *physical*—epilepsy, malaria, opthalmia. The fact that it was a thorn or stake 'in the flesh' would weight the scales in favour of the latter. Whatever it was, we should be grateful for his studied reticence, for we can now confidently apply the divine remedy to our own particular thorn.

We should be grateful, too, that this experience provided the occasion for the enunciation of an important spiritual principle: 'My grace *is* sufficient for you, for my power is made perfect in weakness' (12:9). Here is a divine assurance that even if the painful situation—the thorn, whatever it may be—is not removed, there is always adequate compensating grace available.

This painful and humiliating experience was part of the price of Paul's ministry, part of his equipment for his office. In all probability, in spite of his brilliant gifts, had it not been for the presence of this infirmity he would never have achieved the great work he accomplished.

While we do not know the nature of the thorn, there are certain facts we do know, and they can be of great value in meeting suffering, whether our own or that of others.

1. It was something that continued over a period.

2. It was the subject of repeated, but unanswered prayer. 'Three times I pleaded with the Lord to take it away from me' (v. 8), he stated.

3. It was an instrument of humbling—'to keep me from becoming conceited' (12:7). It deflated his ego and sapped his self-confidence.

4. It afforded Satan the opportunity of tormenting him (12:7). Peter was not the only apostle whom the Lord permitted Satan to sift. The devil meant it for evil, but 'our God turned the curse into a blessing'.

5. It became a channel of grace. 'My grace is sufficient for you'. Rather than remedying it by removal, God gave compensating grace. The answer came, not by subtraction but by addition; not in God granting a more congenial task or a changed location, but in his appropriation of God's more than sufficient grace where and as he was.

6. It provided occasion for rejoicing in weakness. 'Therefore I will boast all the more gladly about my weakness...I delight in weaknesses...For when I am weak, then I am strong' (12:9, 10).

7. It provided a backdrop for displaying Christ's power —'So that Christ's power may rest on me'. In verse 9 the word 'my' should be omitted. Paul's statement is simply,

'power is made perfect in weakness'.

Paul thus mastered the art of turning a debilitating weakness into glorious triumph. He learned that what he had at first regarded as a restricting handicap was in reality a heavenly asset, and the road to an enlarged ministry. Thus his weakness became a potent weapon.

> I asked the Lord that He should give success
> To the high task I sought for Him to do;
> I asked that every hindrance might grow less
> And that my hours of weakness might be few;
> I asked that far and lofty heights be scaled—
> And now I humbly thank Him that I failed.
>
> For with the pain and sorrow came to me
> A dower of tenderness in act and thought,
> And with the failure came a sympathy,
> An insight which success had never brought.
> Father, I had been foolish and unblest
> If Thou hadst granted me my blind request.
>
> *Anon*

Paul's attitude to this disciplinary experience was exemplary. Note that he did not say, 'A thorn was *imposed* on me', but 'there was *given* me'–as a gift of grace. By the time it came to him it was no longer a messenger of Satan to torment him, but a gift of God's grace to prepare the way for a wider ministry.

Concerning time

Time is the leader's most precious commodity, and his use of it will determine not only the amount of work achieved, but also its quality.

Time is not given, but purchased. Some such thought lies behind Paul's cryptic words, 'Redeeming the time', or 'Buy up the opportunities', as Weymouth has it (Eph 5:16).

Time is opportunity, and it becomes ours only by purchase. There is a price to be paid for its most strategic employment. We exchange our time in the market of life for certain occupations or activities. J. B. Phillips adds another angle: 'Make the best use of your time', i.e. exchange it only for things of greatest value.

Time is a stewardship of which we must render account. On its strategic use will depend the value of our contribution to our generation. Each moment is a gift of God and therefore should not be wasted. Because it is our most valuable possession, we should develop a critical conscience in this area.

Time can be lost as well as redeemed, and it is a sobering thought to remember that lost time can never be recalled. Nor can time be hoarded, it must be fully spent each day. It cannot be postponed, it is now or never. If it is not used productively, it is irretrievably lost.

Paul's mastery of time can be measured by the amount he achieved in his lifetime. To follow his extensive journeys on the map, to fit in all his ministry and work leaves one almost breathless. If we, too, are to experience successful leadership, the mastery of *our* time will be a matter of prime importance. Like his Master, Paul selected his priorities with great care, allowing no time for things that were not vital. His life demonstrated that strength of moral character develops through refusing the unimportant.

In this over-heated and over-pressured age, it is instructive to notice that the Apostle seemed to accept pressures and interruptions as normal routine. And few things generate more pressures than those caused by insufficient time.

'We do not want you to be uninformed, brothers,' he wrote, 'about the hardships we suffered in the province of Asia. *We were under great pressure* ... so that we despaired even of life. Indeed, in our hearts we felt the sentence of death' (2 Cor 1:8, 9). He realized that in his God-planned life these things had been foreseen, and they need not disturb him. To the alert Christian, interruptions are divinely interjected opportunities. And Paul was convinced that his life had been divinely planned: 'We are God's workmanship, created in Christ Jesus to do good works, which God prepared in advance for us to do' (Eph 2:10). It is blessedly possible for us through prayer and communion to discover the unfolding pattern for each day.

In seeking to plan our time to the best advantage, it may be helpful to bear the following suggestions in mind:

Everyone has been entrusted with the same amount of time.

God's plan will leave sufficient time for the fulfilment of all His will for that day.

He will expect of us for any day only what is reasonable and within our capabilities.

When we select our priorities carefully, they need not conflict with our obvious duties.

The conflicts and pressures we experience usually arise through our confusing human desires or pressures—our own or those of someone else—with the duties God expects us to fulfil.

Time is too valuable to be spent on secondary matters when primary matters are screaming for attention. 'I didn't have time' is usually the unconscious confession of someone who is making a wrong choice of priorities.

Few things bring the conscientious Christian worker into bondage more thoroughly than this matter of the strategic employment of his time, for it seems to be perennially in short supply. It is necessary, therefore, either to come to terms with it, or to work under perpetual tension and strain. After all, there will always be great areas of unmet need, even after we have conscientiously done all in our power to meet our obligations. By careful and prayerful selection of priorities *we should make each half hour carry its own quota of usefulness*, and then commit the rest to God. Our real problem is not in the *amount* of time available, but in its strategic employment, and for this we alone are responsible. It will involve firm purpose and strict self-discipline but it can be done if we will.

Our responsibility extends only to those things which lie within our own control. Every call for help is not necessarily a call from God. It is manifestly impossible to respond to every appeal for aid. Circumstances beyond our control are no cause for self-accusation.

The leader should, however, honestly face the question, 'Am I using my time doing what matters most, or am I dissipating some of it on matters of secondary importance?' The best way to answer the question is to conduct a strict analysis of the way in which we fill our time in any one week. The exercise might bring some surprises.

Paul challenged the Corinthians, 'Follow my example, as I follow the example of Christ' (1 Cor 11:1), a challenge few of us would care to throw out. In his use of time, he modelled his life on his Lord, and how much both managed to crowd into the days!

Taking time for disciplined recreation and relaxation should not be regarded as a matter of secondary importance. The leader who makes provision for the renewal of physical and nervous resources is not triflingly employed. Jesus took His disciples aside for rest and relaxation. He Himself sat down and rested on the well when He was weary after busy ministry. He did not flog His tired body relentlessly on. Had He done so, He would have missed the prepared heart of the needy woman. Jesus was not an ascetic who refused to enter into the normal social life of the people. He did not consider it time wasted when He attended the wedding feast.

Failure to take adequate time for relaxation may prove counter-productive. Of course, we must always be ready to have our recreation time broken into if the interests of the Kingdom so demand. It must always be, 'First the Kingdom of God'.

When the saintly young revivalist, Robert Murray McCheyne, lay on his death-bed at the age of twenty-nine, he said to the friend sitting with him, 'God gave me a horse to ride and a message to deliver. Alas, I have killed the horse, and now I cannot deliver the message!' There is no virtue in flogging the horse unmercifully. But perhaps that is not our trouble. Maybe our horse needs spurs!

A perusal of the Gospels leaves one with the impression that the Master walked through life with a measured and unhurried tread. He never seemed harassed although he was perpetually thronged. He managed to make people feel He had time for everyone.

Wherein lay the secret of His serenity? I believe it lay in His assurance that He was walking in step with His Father's time-plan—a plan drawn so accurately that every hour was accounted for. He allowed no one to advance or retard His time-schedule. He arranged His calendar each day in communion with His Father. Each day He received the words He should say and the works He should do, and this made Him serene in the midst of crowding duties. 'The words I say to you are not just my own. Rather, it is the Father, living in me, who is doing his work' (Jn 14:10).

Jesus moved in the consciousness that there was a divine timing for the events of His life, and His concern was to complete the task committed to Him in the allotted time. When His brothers were pressing Him to publicize Himself, He made a revealing statement: 'The right time for me has not yet come; for you any time is right' (Jn 7:6). He refused to live a haphazard life, as that would mar His Father's plan. Paul modelled his life on that of His Master, and so should we.

But to effect a radical change in our time habits will require dependence on the Lord's enabling. Not all of us have inflexible wills as Paul appeared to have, but we can all be 'strengthened with might in the inner man' for this purpose. He gave Timothy the helpful assurance that 'God did not give us a spirit of timidity, but a spirit of power, of love and of *self-discipline'* (2 Tim 1:7). A. T. Robertson says that this refers to the human spirit as endowed by the Holy Spirit, on whose cooperation we can count.

The use of our time depends on the pressure of motive. Is our motivation sufficiently compelling to counter our erroneous and long-indulged time habits?

10

Paul and the Role of Women

Since women constitute considerably more than one half of the membership of the universal Church, an understanding of Paul's view of the role of women in the Church is of vital importance. With the rise of the women's liberation movement whose basis is cultural rather than biblical, attitudes have become more strongly polarized than ever. In our increasingly egalitarian society it is not easy to view all that the Scriptures have to say on the subject in an objective and unprejudiced manner, for our views have been shaped by long tradition. Probably only in eternity will there be a true consensus.

The problem is the more sensitive because teachers of unquestioned godliness and of comparable scholarship sincerely espouse opposing views. For this reason, undue dogmatism would be out of place, and the author presents his view with due respect for the sincerely held views of those who differ.

This writer takes no extreme position, nor does he contend for a dominant position for women either in the realm of leadership or of theology. He does not believe that because 'there is neither male nor female' in Christ, therefore Scripture recognizes no difference in the roles of men and women in the Church, or that Paul advocated the unisex ideas of our own day. He does believe, however, that there are valid scriptural grounds for women being accorded a much wider and more influential place in the life and ministry of the Church than has traditionally been the case. The subject is too wide for full treatment in the space available but it will be our objective to support this view from Scripture.

In this day of strident contention for women's rights, Paul is often in the firing line, and receives much flak because of his alleged denigration of the role and status of women. 'Maligned on the one hand, exonerated on the other, Paul himself is lost behind a barrage of claim and counterclaim.'[37]

Frequently he is dismissed as a frustrated male chauvinist, venting his spleen on women in general. But those who level these charges against him have either never read the relevant scripture passages carefully and objectively, or have read them with jaundiced eyes, for they will not carry any such interpretation.

It would be difficult to fault Paul in his general attitude to women, marriage and the family. In his contacts with his hostesses, audiences and female members of his team, he is uniformly chivalrous and brotherly. He never hints or asserts any superiority of men over women. In his letters he expresses the highest regard and esteem for his female colleagues, and commends them as his fellow-workers in the gospel without any discrimination between them and male members of the team.

He went far beyond the traditional position accorded to Jewish women, who were segregated and silent in synagogue worship, and upholds their right to pray and prophesy in the church provided their heads were covered. 'Every woman who prays or prophesies with her head uncovered dishonours her head—it is just as though her head were shaved' (1 Cor 11:5). If the relevant texts are read in the context of the times in which they were written, it will be discovered that in his day, far from being a male chauvinist, Paul was a foremost champion of women's rights. He would have been regarded by his contemporaries as distinctly *avant garde*.

In appraising his attitude and teaching, the cultural climate of his times must be kept in view. One need only compare his outlook and practice with those of the leaders and founders of the other great religions to see the great superiority of his conception of the status of women as compared with that of Buddhism, Hinduism and Islam. Instead of denouncing Paul, Christian women should be lauding his championship, for it has paved the way for so many blessings and privileges they now enjoy.

The case has been well stated by George Matheson: 'One of the most distinctive elements in Paul's Christian experience was the recognition of the claims of women; in nothing is he more sharply distinguished from his Jewish countrymen. Even those passages in which he seems to depreciate are dictated by a precisely opposite motive—the desire to conserve for women that distinctive and peculiar sphere of which Jewish politics deprived her.'[38]

In interpreting Paul's teaching on this subject, it should be borne in mind that (a) he was answering specific questions addressed to him by the local church at Corinth, relating to special local problems that were troubling them; (b) he wrote at a time when prevailing conditions were both perilous and precarious. This fact emerges from his answer in 1 Corinthians 7:25,26: 'Now, concerning the unmarried, I have no command of the Lord, but I give my opinion as one who by the Lord's mercy is trustworthy. I think that *in view of the impending distress*, it is well for a man to remain as he is. Are you bound to a wife? Do not seek to be free . . .' etc. and (c) in the Gentile cities where the Christians lived, immorality was rife, and it was most important that Christian women should deport themselves in church in a manner that was above criticism.

It would seem that here he is not legislating for all times and in world terms, but is giving specific advice for the troubled days immediately ahead: in view of present conditions, men would be wise not to change their present state. If this interpretation is correct, and I believe it is, then improved conditions would admit elasticity in implementing his advice.

Where there are clear, unambiguous scriptural statements, they are to be obeyed without reservation. But on this subject the wide divergence of views held by equally sincere persons indicates that they are by no means clear and unambiguous.

On this point J. I.Packer, an evangelical scholar of repute, wrote:

> Though all Paul's commands being apostolic carried the authority of the Lord whose ambassador Paul was, that does not rule out the possibility that some of them were *ad hoc* enactments, responses to particular situations which would become dead letters if the situation changed. It is arguable that the command that women should not teach but keep silent is a case in point: a prudential rule of thumb applying the creation pattern to a situation where converted pagan ladies, uneducated and brought up to think of themselves as inferior beings, had now discovered their dignity under God in Christ, and it was now going to their heads.
>
> In that case it is the principle and not the rule of thumb that has abiding authority, and it is conceivable that under a different cultural background where Christian women were not under the same temptations to wildness, a relaxed rule could serve the principle equally well.'[39]

This principle of interpretation throws light on three important passages concerning which there is a strong polarization of views.

Now I want you to realize that the head of every man is Christ, and the head of the woman is man, and the head of Christ is God. Every man who prays or prophesies with his head covered dishonours his head. And every woman who prays or prophesies with her head uncovered dishonours her head—it is just as though her head were shaved. If a woman does not cover her head, she should have her hair cut off; and if it is a disgrace for a woman to have her hair cut or shaved off, she could cover her head (1 Cor 11:3–6).

For God is not a God of disorder but of peace. As in all the congregations of the saints, women should remain silent in the churches. They are not allowed to speak, but must be in submission, as the Law says. If they want to enquire about something, they should ask their own husbands at home; for it is disgraceful for a woman to speak in the church (1 Cor 14:33–35).

I want men everywhere to lift up holy hands in prayer, without anger or disputing. I also want women to dress modestly, with decency and propriety, not with braided hair or gold or pearls or expensive clothes, but with good deeds, appropriate for women who profess to worship God. A woman should learn in quietness and full submission. I do not permit a woman to teach or to have authority over a man; she must be silent. For Adam was formed first, then Eve. And Adam was not the one deceived; it was the woman who was deceived and became a sinner (1 Tim 2:8–14).

Interpreters on the extreme right maintain that these passages impose an absolute prohibition on any teaching or leadership role for women in the Church, some even going so far as to prohibit their praying at gatherings where men are present. However, the spiritual barrenness and frustration that often results from such an extreme position is a plain matter of fact in past and present church history.

Those on the extreme left interpret the passages as solely reflecting contemporary cultural situations which have no parallel today and are only marginally relevant. They therefore accord to women an unlimited teaching and leadership role in the church.

But are these two extremes the only possible interpretations? May there not be a reasonable alternative position?

Is it not possible that neither is the wholly correct interpretation and that there is an acceptable middle road? Since both Scripture and Paul have so much to say about women, the family and marriage, is it likely that the problem can be resolved by quoting two or three passages, while largely ignoring a much greater body of Scripture? For it is true to say that there has been a rather ill-balanced emphasis on the negative passages quoted above, and inadequate attention paid to many other passages that make a somewhat more liberal interpretation possible.

Paul's lofty conception of the sanctity of the marriage bond is reflected in the parallel he draws between the relation of man and wife to Christ and the Church. 'Husbands, love your wives, just as Christ loved the church and gave himself up for her...' (Eph 5:25). This is in striking contrast to the teaching of the Koran or the Confucian classics in which the emphasis is invariably on the duty of the wife to the husband.

But it was not so with Paul. 'Husbands ought to love their wives as their own bodies. He who loves his wife loves himself' (Eph 5:28,29). It should be noted, too, that the subjection of the woman to the man is 'to her own husband', not to all men.

The question inevitably arises, 'How much should the existing cultural situation in Paul's day be taken into account and influence our contemporary interpretation? In this connection F. F. Bruce makes a pertinent comment: 'Cultural relativity is certainly to be reckoned with when the permanent message of the New Testament receives our practical attention today. The local and temporary situation in which that message was first delivered must be appreciated if we are to discern what its permanent essence really is, and learn to apply it in the local and temporary circumstances of our own culture.'

In 1 Corinthians 11:1–15 Paul is concerned with a question of church order—the advisability of women veiling their heads in public worship services at Corinth, and he is *not volunteering teaching for all time*.

It has been pointed out that the sentence, 'I do not permit a woman to teach or to have authority over a man' appears timeless in English—i.e. 'I never ever allow a woman to teach....' However, in the Greek, it is a present active verb which can be translated, 'I am not presently permitting a woman to teach or to have authority over men.' Paul is apparently prohibiting those who are not properly instructed from teaching. The teacher must first be taught. But the verb tense cannot be made of necessity into a general principle for all time.[40]

What were the cultural conditions prevalent at that time that should be taken into account in our interpretation?

* Almost half the people in the Roman Empire were slaves.
* The status of women was very low. They were mostly unedu-cated and were regarded as chattels.
* In their prayers Jewish men thanked God they were not women.
* Men were not supposed to speak to women in public places.
* An Eastern woman did not go out with her head uncovered. To do so, or to have her head shaved, marked her as immoral.
* In worship in the synagogues they were segregated from the men, and often interrupted by asking their husbands questions which would better be answered at home.

It will be seen that practically none of these cultural conditions find a parallel in the culture of our day. The cross of Christ has effected a vast change in the status of women.

When existing conditions are taken into consideration, the restrictions Paul made were reasonable and necessary. But are they equally applicable in the cultural climate of our own times? What were guiding lines for worshippers in one church and cultural situation should not be turned into binding laws for all time and all situations.

Paul's restrictions were aimed at correcting improprieties, and to bring order in very disturbed church gatherings (1 Cor 14:33), not to place a blanket ban on women praying, prophesying, evangelizing or teaching. His emphasis is upon women conducting themselves so blamelessly that their behaviour will neither disrupt the worship nor shame their husbands. He is discouraging public questioning or arguing, where wives were usurping authority over their husbands and thus disgracing them.

While admitting the undoubtedly difficult problems of interpretation of these passages, there are other considerations that make it doubtful whether the traditionally negative attitude is the true and only possible explanation.

The Holy Spirit sovereignly bestows spiritual gifts on each believer without reference to gender (1 Cor 12:11). These gifts are stated to be used for the upbuilding of the Church. Had He withheld these gifts of teaching or leadership from women, we would accept that as a clear indication of His will. But He has not done so. If men only are appointed to positions where these gifts may be exercised, is not the purpose of the Spirit's gift being frustrated and the Church impoverished?

'The Spirit of God has expressly endowed some women in both the Old and New Testaments with powers of leadership, as though to show that He reserves this right, even though the vast majority of leaders have been men.'[41]

Both Old and New Testaments and church history past and present provide examples of godly women exercising a fruitful ministry in prophecy, administration, evangelism and teaching. Where there is a wooden adherence to the prohibitions in today's changed situation, sterility and frustration very often result. On the other hand, the undoubted spiritual release and fruitfulness that has followed the ministry of such women as Catherine Booth, Ruth Paxson, Henrietta Meares, Geraldine Howard Taylor, Isabel Kuhn and many others has to be accounted for if the negative interpretation is the correct one.

It is true that the New Testament does not depict women in a dominant role in theology or leadership, but there is a great deal short of those roles that they did in the early church and may still do—often better than men.

Hudson Taylor was a pioneer not only in the use of lay people in missionary work, but also in the use of single women in pioneer work in China. In 1885 the China Inland Mission opened centres on the populous Kwang Sin River that were conducted by single women. Thirty years later there was a complete chain of 10 central stations, 60 out-stations, over 2,200 communicants and large numbers of enquirers, pupils in schools etc. Those ladies were still the only foreign missionaries alongside the native pastors whom they had trained.

In view of this remarkable achievement, one cannot but ask, 'Does the Holy Spirit speak with two voices—bidding women not to teach or lead, and then richly blessing them when they disobey?' If it is objected, 'But we must go by Scripture and not by experience', the objection is valid; but it must be *Scripture rightly interpreted*, and in this case the presumption surely is that this is not the correct interpretation. More than 60 per cent of missionaries today are women, most of whom exercise functions which the extreme position would deny them. Without their contribution in teaching and often in leadership, the missionary cause would be immeasurably impoverished.

Paul apparently saw no discrepancy between the instructions he gave, and the fact that in his times women did pray, prophesy, teach and evangelize. He numbered many women among his friends and fellow-workers, and was warm in his praise and appreciation of their sacrificial service.

In Romans 16 he gives special mention to almost as many women as men friends, and the expressions he uses throw some light on their role and ministry in those early days of the Church.

Phoebe (vv.1,2) is described as 'deacon'. In the Greek the word 'deacon' is the same whether in masculine or feminine gender. It is the same word as Paul used of himself and Apollos (1 Cor 3:5), and there are no linguistic or theological grounds for differentiating between her function and that of other male deacons. The word is used as often of women as of men. As D. G. Stewart commented, it seems that women were doing as much of the work of a deacon as men, whether they were given the title or not.

In verse 2 the word translated 'helper' further elucidates her function. Cognate terms from the same root are applied to those who exercised leadership in the churches, e.g. 'those who are over you in the Lord' (1 Thess 5:12). In Romans 12:8 it is rendered 'leader' and in 1 Timothy 5:17 it is applied to 'the elders who direct the affairs of the church'. So the term Paul uses could indicate that Phoebe not only filled the function of a deacon, but also had some administrative role.

Priscilla (v.3) appears to have been more dynamic than her husband Aquila, but together they functioned as a husband-wife pastoral team who conducted a church in their home in Corinth and Rome. That she exercised a teaching ministry is explicit in Scripture (Acts 18:26), where she and her husband are stated to have taken the eloquent Apollos to their home and explained the way of God more adequately. There is no suggestion that in doing so she was acting contrary to Paul's teaching. She shared with Aquila the title and task of a 'fellow-worker'. Paul asserts the indebtedness of 'all the churches of the Gentiles' to their joint ministry.

Junias or Junia (v.7) was stated to be a woman by both Chrysostom and Theophylact. Ancient commentators regarded Andronicus and Junias as a married couple. Junias is not found elsewhere as a man's name. Of Junia Chrysostom wrote: 'And indeed to be apostles at all is a great thing. But to be even among these of note just consider what a great encomium this is. But they were of note owing to their works, to their achievements. Oh! how great is the devotion of this woman, that she should be even counted worthy of the appellation of apostle.'[42]

Instead of the rendering 'men of note among the apostles' (v.7 RSV), in the NIV it is rendered, 'they were outstanding among the apostles', using that word, of course, in its secondary sense, as of Barnabas.

So while there is no absolute certainty, there are reasonable grounds for regarding Junia as an apostle in the limited sense.

Philip's daughters (Acts 21:9) were referred to by Eusebius as 'mighty luminaries'. They exercised the prophetic gift. In 1 Corinthians 11:5 Paul gave instructions concerning women's attire when praying or prophesying, and in that context there is no distinction made between the praying and prophesying of the men (v.4) and the women (v.5). In each place where Paul lists spiritual gifts, prophecy is given the prime position as the most important gift, and in 1 Corinthians 14:3 he specifies its nature and function: 'Everyone who prophesies speaks to men for their strengthening, encouragement and comfort'. Would it not be strange if Paul permitted women to exercise the higher gift of prophecy, yet forbade the less important gift of teaching?

Euodia and Syntyche (Phil 4:2,3) apparently held positions of leadership in the church so influential that their disagreement endangered its unity. While not condoning their estrangement, Paul commends them most warmly. 'They contended at my side in the cause of the gospel', sharing the common task and ministry. He identifies them with Clement and the other fellow-workers in the proclamation of the gospel.

From these instances there is a good case for maintaining that even in the early Church, the command to keep silence was not absolute, nor were women precluded from exercising a fruitful and fulfilling ministry.

In 2 Timothy 2:2 Paul wrote: 'The things you have heard me say in the presence of many witnesses entrust to reliable men who will also be qualified to teach others.' In point of fact 'men' here is a generic term and could be equally rendered 'faithful persons', a term that could include women.

'That some women today have a gift for teaching and applying the Bible can hardly be denied. This would seem to be one measure of the difference between our situation and Paul's when there was no N.T. to teach! But the giving of the gift is itself an indication that God meant the gift to be used in the Church for edification. *Prima facie*, then, God intends some women to teach and preach.'[43]

In the light of what has been written, Paul appears to accord to women a satisfying if not dominant role in the realms of prayer, teaching, evangelizing and administration. As stated earlier, there is no scriptural precedent for women holding a dominant role in leadership or in theology, but in His administration of the Church and the execution of the Great Commission the Holy Spirit has given a much wider scope of ministry to women than is usually accorded to them in our churches. Is there a valid reason for our being more selective than the Holy Spirit?

11

Paul's Philosophy of Weakness

We form part of a generation that worships power—military, intellectual, economic, scientific. The concept of power is worked into the warp and woof of our daily living. Our world is divided into power blocs. Men everywhere are striving for power in various realms, often with questionable motivation.

On no subject is there a more stark and startling contrast between God's outlook and our own. His words through Isaiah in his day are no less appropriate in our own: 'My thoughts are not your thoughts, neither are your ways my ways' (Is 55:8). Unlike every other worldly philosophy, the gospel seeks out the weak and the poor.

The celebrated Scottish preacher James S. Stewart made a statement that is both revolutionary and challenging, because it strikes such a shrewd blow at our human pride and self-sufficiency.

> It is always upon human weakness and humiliation, not human strength and confidence, that God chooses to build His Kingdom; and he can use us not merely in spite of our ordinariness and helplessness and disqualifying infirmities, but precisely because of them. It is a thrilling discovery to make, and it can revolutionise our missionary outlook.[44]

These words are indeed revolutionary, but no more so than Paul's own, for Dr Stewart is entirely in sympathy with Paul's philosophy of weakness. Note some of his paradoxical statements:

> God chose the weak things of the world to shame the strong (1 Cor 1:27).

> I came to you in weakness and fear, and with much trembling (1 Cor 2:3)

> I delight in weaknesses... for when I am weak, then I am strong (2 Cor 12:10).

> My power is made perfect in weakness (2 Cor 12:9).

> I will not boast about myself, except about my weaknesses (2 Cor 12:5).

These surprising passages enshrine one of the master principles of Paul's leadership, as they should of ours. It completely reverses the thinking of the worldly mind and challenges accepted standards. Who would consider weakness a leadership quality? But Paul had learned that 'the foolishness of God'—activities that seem foolish to the unregenerate—'is wiser than man's vaunted wisdom, and the weakness of God'—operations of God that to men seem weak and futile—'is stronger than man's strength' (1 Cor 1:25).

God is a God who hides Himself, and His power is usually hidden power. He often conceals His omnipotence under a mantle of silence. Who notices the tons of sap being forced through the wood of the great tree trunk? How silently and unnoticed water becomes ice! His weakness is greater than our power.

The hidden wisdom and power of God is seen, Paul says, in the kind of people He chooses to establish His Kingdom.

Not many of you were wise by human standards; not many were influential; not many were of noble birth. But God chose the foolish things of the world to shame the wise...so that no one may boast before him (1 Cor 1:26–29).

'It must not be forgotten', wrote A. T. Robertson, 'that Jesus chose His disciples from the unschooled artisans and fishermen of Galilee save Judas the Judean. He passed by the rabbinical theological seminaries where religious impulse had died and thought had crystallised. He will pass by the schools of today if the teachers and students close their minds to Him.'[45]

Paul, although himself an intellectual, gloried in the fact that God had purposefully chosen, not so much the highly intellectual or highly born or powerful and influential, as people who were weak in gift and influence—often those weak in body, and even the nonentities—through whom to achieve His purposes of blessing. And the reason for His choice? 'That no one may boast before Him'.

Dr Stewart sees in our very human weaknesses a potentially powerful divine weapon: 'Nothing can defeat a church or soul that takes not its strength but its weakness, and offers that to be God's weapon. It was the way of William Carey and Francis Xavier and Paul the apostle. "Lord, here is my human weakness: I dedicate it to Thee for Thy glory!" This is the strategy to which there is no retort. This is the victory that overcomes the world'.[46]

So with the Lord; he takes and He refuses,
    Finds Him ambassadors whom men deny,
Wise ones nor mighty for His saints He chooses,
    No such as John, or Gideon or I.

Ay, for this Paul, a scorn and a despising,
    Weak as you know him, and the wretch you see—

Even in these eyes shall ye behold him rising,
Strength in infirmities, and Christ in me.

F. W. H. Myers

Of course God does not confine Himself to weak and despised nonentities! The Countess of Huntingdon, referring to 1 Corinthians 1:26 used to say, 'I am so thankful for one letter in the Bible; it does not say not *any* noble, but not *many* noble'. God wants to bless and use all His children irrespective of accidents of birth, native talent, charm of disposition. But He can do so only when they are willing to renounce dependence on their merely natural gifts and qualifications.

It is Paul's contention that God can achieve His purpose most completely either in the absence of human wisdom and power and resources, or where there is abandonment of reliance on them. Human weakness provides the best background for the display of God's power.

Paul himself was one of the wise, noble, and influential men of his day. He possessed intellectual power, emotional ardour, fiery zeal and irresistible logic, and yet he renounced reliance on these and all the other artifices at his command. Note the spirit in which he approached his ministry to the Corinthian church:

> I came to you in weakness and fear, and with much trembling. My message and my preaching were not with wise and persuasive words, but with a demonstration of the Spirit's power (1 Cor 2:3,4).

Even while making use of his gifts and qualifications, he inwardly renounced dependence on them to achieve spiritual results and relied on the ungrieved Holy Spirit to supply the power. He welcomed the weakness that made his dependence on God more complete.

Dwight L. Moody, the Billy Graham of his day, learned

to exploit the power of weakness as Paul did. He was lacking in education, his physical appearance was unattractive, and his voice was high-pitched and nasal. But his conscious weakness did not prevent God from shaking the world through him.

On one occasion a press reporter was assigned to cover his campaigns and to discover the secret of his extraordinary power and influence over people of all strata of society. When he turned in his report he wrote: 'I can see nothing whatever in Moody to account for his marvellous work.'

When Moody was told this, he chuckled, 'Of course not, because the work was God's, not mine.' Moody's weakness was God's weapon.

Paul's 'thorn in the flesh' was a perpetual reminder of his human weakness, but he realized it was not purposeless—it was 'so that the power of Christ might rest on him'.

James Denney wrote in this connection: 'No one who saw this [power] and looked at a preacher like Paul, could dream the explanation lay in him. Not in an ugly little Jew, without presence, without eloquence, without the means to bribe or to compel, could the source of such courage, the source of such transformations, be found; it must be sought, not in him but in God.'[47]

It is unlikely that Paul displayed his weakness from the beginning of his ministry. Like us, he was disposed to protest, and it was a gradual educative process. '*I have learned* to be content whatever the circumstances' (Phil 4:11). But as he mastered the divine law of compensation, he ultimately reached the high ground of being able to say in sincerity, '*I delight in weaknesses*, in insults, in hardships, in persecutions, in difficulties. For when I am weak, then I am strong' (2 Cor 12:10).

One great secret of his success as a leader was that he set his followers a glowing example of extracting power from his weaknesses. He wrested their secret from them, and through the Spirit's ministry discovered that they could become a source of strength instead of weakness.

Are we not inclined to regard our weakness and inadequacy as a justifiable excuse for shrinking from the difficult assignment? God advances these very qualities as reasons for tackling it. If we maintain that we are too weak, He asserts that as the very reason He chose us, so that His strength can be perfected in our weakness. It was said of the heroes of faith of Hebrews 11 that 'out of weakness they were made strong' (v.34).

At the very beginning of the China Inland Mission in January 1866, Hudson Taylor expressed his philosophy of weakness in the C.I.M. Occasional Paper No. 1.

'We may adopt the language of the Apostle Paul, and say, "Who is sufficient for these things?" Utter weakness in ourselves, we should be overwhelmed with the immensity of the work before us, and the weight of responsibility lying upon us, were it not that our very weakness and insufficiency gives us special claim to the fulfilment of HIS promise who has said, "My grace is sufficient for thee; my strength is made perfect in weakness."'

One hundred and eighteen years later, the mission he founded, now the Overseas Missionary Fellowship, is still proving the validity of this philosophy.

12

Paul Training a Leader

It was John R. Mott's contention that leaders must seek to multiply their lives by developing younger men, by giving them full play and adequate outlet for their powers. In order to achieve that, heavy burdens of responsibility should be laid on them, including increasing opportunities of initiative and power of final decision. They should be given recognition and generous credit for their achievements.

Paul's method of preparing Timothy for his life-work was deeply instructive. He trod in the steps of his Master, and his techniques were fully in harmony with Mott's prescription. He poured his own personality and convictions into him, and was prepared to spend much time with him.

Timothy would be about twenty years of age when his tutelage began. He had been brought up in a feminine atmosphere—his father may have died—and a tendency to effeminacy was probably accentuated by his own indifferent health. 'He was more prone to lean than to lead.' His innate timidity and tendency to self-pity, too, needed correction and more iron needed to be built into his character. From incidental references it could be inferred that he could be overtolerant and partial with important people, and tended to be desultory about his work.

From Paul's exhortation to 'stir up the gift' it appears that like many others, he was apt to rely on old spiritual experiences instead of rekindling their dying flame.

In spite of these minuses in his make-up, Paul cherished a high opinion of his potential and had very lofty and exacting aspirations for him. He held him to the highest and did not spare him difficult experiences. Nor did he shelter him from hardships that would toughen his fibre and impart virility. He assigned him tasks far above his conscious ability, but encouraged and fortified him in their execution. How else could a young man develop his powers and capacities than by tackling situations that extended him to the limit?

A great deal of Timothy's training was received on the job, as he travelled with Paul—a unique privilege for so young a man. He would come into contact with men of all kinds, men of stature whose personalities and achievements would kindle in him a wholesome ambition. From his tutor he would learn how to meet triumphantly the reverses and crises that seemed routine in Paul's life and ministry.

He was allowed to share the ministry with his colleagues. Paul entrusted him with responsibility for establishing the Christian nucleus at Thessalonica and confirming them in the faith, a task for which he earned Paul's approval. He was sent as trouble-shooter to Corinth—a hot spot where Paul's apostolic authority was under fire. He may have failed, but he learned invaluable lessons in the process. As is usually the case, Paul's exacting standards, high expectations and heavy demands served to bring out the best in the young man and saved him from the peril of mediocrity.

'Great men are made more by their failures than by their successes.' 'Abraham Lincoln is perhaps the best-known example. He was a failure in business; he was a failure as a lawyer; he failed to become a candidate for the State legislature. He was thwarted in his attempt to become commissioner of the General Land Office. He was defeated in his bids for the vice-presidency and Senate. But he didn't let failure ruin his life. Nor did he allow failure to embitter him toward people.'

In a day when a man of under thirty years of age was not considered worthy of much notice, Timothy's youthfulness was a distinct handicap. But that did not stop Paul giving him early responsibility and encouraging him not to be dismayed because of it.

'Don't let anyone look down on you because you are young', he counselled, 'but set an example for the believers in speech, in life, in love, in faith and in purity' (1 Tim 4:12). These are qualities in which youth is apt to be deficient. Exemplary living could largely offset the disadvantage of youthfulness. A young man said to the author at a centre of Christian work, 'You have to have gray hair to give out a hymn-book here!' The secretary of the movement was over eighty! Paul teaches the important lesson that it is wise to entrust promising and stable young people with reasonable responsibility earlier rather than later.

Paul's charge

Paul concentrated his counsel to Timothy in a fourfold charge.

In order to encourage and fortify the young pastor for his daunting task at Ephesus, a church that had enjoyed a galaxy of talent, and for which he would feel utterly inadequate, Paul addressed four solemn charges to him, from which we can learn what things he deemed most important in pastoral work.

Guard the deposit

'Timothy, guard what has been entrusted to your care. Turn away from godless chatter and the opposing ideas of what is falsely called knowledge, which some have professed and in so doing have wandered from the faith' (1 Tim 6:20, 21).

Moffat translates this as 'Keep the securities of the faith intact'. This is a banking illustration, and the word sometimes translated as 'deposit' has much the same significance as today—money entrusted to a banker for safe-keeping. It is the duty of the banker to hand it back intact. Paul is saying to Timothy, 'God has made a deposit in your bank; stand guard over it'.

Timothy had been entrusted with God's salvation truths, and he would have to give an account of his stewardship. He must use his spiritual gifts to the best possible advantage in advancing the Kingdom. He had been appointed a herald, and must therefore sound out the Word: 'Of this gospel I have been made a herald', he claimed, and in proclaiming it he must be sure to keep the deposit intact. He must defend the faith against the attacks of false teachers, as well as preaching it positively.

In our justifiable reaction to an unloving fundamentalism that has betrayed its cause by vitriolic attacks on personalities, we must not become so tolerant that we fail to guard the deposit. It is possible to contend for the faith without being contentious in spirit.

Act without favouritism

'I charge you, in the sight of God and Christ Jesus and the elect angels, to keep these instructions without partiality, and to do nothing out of favouritism' (1 Tim 5:21). Did this charge spring from Paul's fear that young Timothy might be too easily influenced by pressure groups—a situation which is not unknown in Christian work in our own day?

We are all liable to be moved by subjective considerations, and need the stiffening this grave charge would afford. In Christian work absolute impartiality and unimpeachable honesty and integrity are essential. Our own aversions or affinities must be laid aside. The words 'partiality' and 'favouritism' both imply prejudice—a prejudging of the case. Even worldly men expect fairness and impartiality, and the Church should set the standard, since its wellbeing is dependent on an impartial discipline.

Keep the principles stainless

'I charge you to keep this commandment without spot or blame until the appearing of our Lord Jesus Christ, which God will bring about in his own time' (1 Tim 6:13–15).

The word 'keep' means to preserve, to stand guard over. It would seem that Paul was urging Timothy to keep the commission entrusted to him, the principles enshrined in the word of God, unsullied and flawless until the appearing of Christ. The leader is guardian of the principles of the church, mission or organization in which he carries responsibility. It is for him to practise, teach and cherish them and see that they are conscientiously observed by those under his care.

Keep your sense of urgency

'In the presence of God and of Jesus Christ, who will judge the living and the dead, and in view of his appearing and his kingdom, I give you this charge: Preach the Word; be prepared in season and out of season; correct, rebuke and encourage' (2 Tim 4:1, 2). It should be borne in mind that Paul was anticipating his early demise, and was therefore more than usually under the influence of the world to come. His charge would be especially solemn to his young colleague.

'Preach the word—proclaim it in all its glory and completeness', he urged. 'Be ready whether the opportunity seems favourable or unfavourable, convenient or inconvenient. Buy up every opportunity. Never lose your sense of urgency. Take the initiative and press forward with unflagging zeal'.

The old warrior had earned the right to pass on these charges to the younger man, for he had demonstrated them to a unique degree in his own life and ministry.

Trustworthy sayings

In pastoral letters Paul wrote to encourage and brace Timothy, he recounts five 'trustworthy sayings', each of which deals with important aspects of Christian life and service. By using the formula: 'Here is a trustworthy saying that deserves full acceptance', he was drawing attention to sayings which apparently were current in the churches of their day, and they are still contemporary.

Salvation

'Here is a trustworthy saying that deserves full acceptance: Christ Jesus came into the world to save sinners—of whom I am the worst' (1 Tim 1:15).

This saying which epitomizes the gospel is a startling but simple epigram that has stood the fiery test of challenge and experience. It has emerged from the crucible of ridicule and persecution with lustre undimmed, and should therefore command spontaneous and enthusiastic assent.

Paul here uses the expression, 'came into the world', not merely to express change of location, but change of state and environment. The supreme sacrifice is implied—'to save sinners'. The more he grasped the magnitude of the sacrifice of Christ and the grace of God, the deeper his consciousness of his own unworthiness—'of whom I am the worst'.

Leadership

'Here is a trustworthy saying: If anyone sets his heart on being an overseer, he desires a noble task' (1 Tim 3:1). The New English Bible renders it: 'To aspire to leadership is a noble ambition'. It should be noted that the nobility is in the task itself, and not in the prestige it may confer.

It may well be asked, 'But does not this saying tend to encourage unworthy or sinful ambition—"the last infirmity of noble minds?"' Should not the office seek the man, rather than the man the office?

Yes and no! Today, the office of bishop or overseer is prestigious, but when Paul wrote these words, it involved a great degree of sacrifice and danger. To assume this office in the church was to invite persecution, hardship and even death—even as it does in some lands today. This would surely tend to choke off the wrong types.

Under the circumstances existing in those days, strong incentive was needed to encourage the right type of person to take office, and Paul was seeking to provide this.

Sanctification

He saved us through the washing of re-birth and renewal by the Holy Spirit, whom he poured out on us generously through Jesus Christ our Saviour, so that, having been justified by his grace, we might become heirs having hope of eteral life. This is a trustworthy saying and I want you to stress these things (Tit 3:5–8).

What were the things the young leader was to stress? (a) The philanthropy of God (v. 4)—His unfailing goodness and lovingkindness. This stands out in stark contrast to the inhumanity of man in verse 3, and highlights the darkness of their past with the light of their present experience; (b) the regenerating and renewing power of the Holy Spirit (v. 5); (c) the grace of Christ in associating us as heirs with Himself (v. 7). As a result of this action of the Trinity, we have the hope of eternal life; (d) the Holy Spirit is not doled out with a niggardly hand but is 'poured out generously' (v. 6). Titus must proclaim these truths with all certainty.

Suffering

'Here is a trustworthy saying: If we died with him, we will also live with him; if we endure, we will also reign with him; if we disown him, he will also disown us; if we are faithless, he will remain faithful, for he cannot disown himself' (2 Tim 2:11–13).

This was one of the hymns of the early Church. It emphasizes the fact that the Church is heir to the Cross. In the troubled days in which we live, when violence and revolution seem endemic, our teaching should prepare people for such situations as Christians are facing in many countries. Luther wrote, 'If we are put to death out of loyalty to Christ, we shall also live with him in glory'.

Loyalty to Christ will be rewarded and disloyalty will bring its own retribution. If we choose to die to earthly ease and advantage for His sake, there will be heavenly compensations. Tertullian claimed that the person who is afraid to suffer cannot belong to Him who has suffered.

How glad we should be that there are some things God cannot do—'He cannot disown himself'.

Self-discipline

'Train yourself to be godly. For physical training is of some value, but godliness has value for all things, holding promise for both the present life and the life to come. This is a trustworthy saying that deserves full acceptance.' (1 Tim 4:7–9).

The picture in these verses is of a gymnasium where the athletic youth trained for the arena. Paul exhorts Timothy not to confine himself merely to pious meditation, but to exercise himself vigorously in godly living. The passage breathes strenuousness and discipline. The athlete spares no effort or self-denial in order to win the prize. He discards everything that impedes progress, and so should the Christian athlete. Moral muscle and spiritual sinew come from serious exercise in the realm of the Spirit, and will pay handsome dividends in the life to come.

Physical discipline and exercise is valuable, but when compared with spiritual discipline, its benefits are limited. One results in beauty of physique, the other in life everlasting. One concerns this present time, the other impinges on eternity. Physical training should not be disparaged, however, for the body is the temple of the Holy Spirit.

Stir up the Gift

At his ordination, Paul and the elders laid their hands on Timothy and he received the grace-gift of the Spirit which would equip him as apostolic representative. Aware of his weakness, Paul gave him a double exhortation.

'*Do not neglect your gift,* which was given you through a prophetic message when the body of elders laid their hands on you' (1 Tim 4:14). Don't grow careless of the sacred trust! It was a sovereignly bestowed endowment of the Spirit—not an external operation but an inward grace. Apparently the efficiency of the gift was not automatic—it could decline. 'Don't let it suffer by neglect' was the advice.

'*Fan into flame the gift* of God, which is in you through the laying on of my hands. For God did not give us a spirit of timidity, but a spirit of power, of love and of self-discipline' (2 Tim 1:6, 7). It was not that he required a new endowment. 'Stir up that inner fire' is J. B. Phillips' rendering. The fire had burned low.

Did Paul sense that Timothy's zeal had begun to wane? Flame doesn't automatically rise higher, it tends to die down. In Timothy's case there was so much to quench the flame. 'Keep in full flame' or 'rekindle' the fire if it has died down! Place fresh fuel on the dying embers!

Paul challenges and stimulates Timothy by directing his attention to the nature of the divine endowment. The *charisma* gift of verse 6 goes along with the *pneuma* Spirit of verse 7.

We may well ask ourselves: have we been neglecting the gift? Is the flame burning low in our lives? Does it need stirring up?

13

Straining Towards the Tape

In spite of all his achievements and successes, Paul was by no means self-confident. He had no doubt as to his own salvation, but he was painfully alive to the possibility of being disqualified in the race and not reaching the tape. So he practised constant self-mastery: 'I beat my body and make it my slave so that after I have preached to others, I myself will not be disqualified for the prize' (1 Cor 9:27).

He was no stranger to the inside of a prison. His visit to Jerusalem (Acts 21:17) in about AD 58 resulted in a five-year imprisonment—painful and wearisome for him but abundantly fruitful for the Church. It was a case of 'out of the eater came forth meat, and out of the strong... sweetness'. It proved to be anything but lost time, and resulted in the enrichment of the Church and the world for the ensuing centuries.

The story reveals how human malice is controlled by divine sovereignty. The Jews wanted the prisoner transferred from Caesarea to Jerusalem. Had Festus acceded to their demands, the New Testament may not have had Ephesians, Philippians, Colossians and Pilemon.

His appeal to Caesar (Acts 25:11) led to two years of imprisonment in Rome where he enjoyed a measure of liberty. It is to this period we owe 1 and 2 Timothy and Titus. What seem at the time to be tragedies often prove, in the long run, to be triumphs. It was when John was in a concentration camp that he wrote the Apocalypse. While in Bedford Jail Bunyan wrote his immortal *The Pilgrim's Progress*.

The manner in which Paul turned even his misfortunes to account should encourage those who are 'prisoners' through ill-health or other circumstances, to be ingenious in seeking ways in which they can use the restricting circumstances to good account.

> Blessed is he whose faith is not offended,
>   When all around his way
> The power of God is working out deliverance
>   For others day by day.
>
> Though in some prison drear his own soul languish
>   Till life be spent
> Yet still can trust his father's love and purpose,
>   And rest therein content.
>
> Yea, blessed art thou, whose faith is not offended
>   By trials unexplained,
> By mysteries unsolved, past understanding,
>   Until the goal is gained.

F. H. Allen

Paul is now about to hand on the torch to young Timothy. 'But you, keep your head in all situations' he writes. 'Endure hardship, do the work of an evangelist, discharge all the duties of your ministry. For I am already being poured out like a drink offering, and the time has come for my departure. I have fought the good fight, I have finished the race, I have kept the faith. Now there is in store for me the crown of righteousness which the Lord, the righteous Judge, will award to me on that day' (2 Tim 4:5-7).

Because his own was drawing to a close, he urged Timothy to fulfil his ministry at whatever cost to himself. The Greek word for 'departure' is used of loosing the moorings of a boat. He was casting off the shore-lines and was about to embark for the heavenly shore, but he could do it with a sense of 'mission accomplished'. What a model for Timothy—and for us. The torch is now in our hands.

Mission accomplished

Tradition has it that, as a result of his appeal to Nero, after two trials in AD 68, Paul was put to death.

The Emperor, it is reported, went on a trip while Paul was in Rome, during which one of his favourite mistresses was won to the Lord by Paul. When Nero arrived home, she was gone, having joined a Christian group. Nero was so infuriated that he wreaked his vengeance on Paul. They took him out to the Ostian way and executed him.

> Yea, through life, death, thro' sorrow and
>   thro' winning,
>   He shall suffice me, for He hath sufficed:
> Christ is the end, for Christ is the beginning,
>   Christ the beginning, for the end is Christ.

F. W. H. Myers

Notes

Preface

[1] Frederick W. H. Myers, *Saint Paul* (London, MacMillan, 1910).

Chapter 1

[2] *Newsweek*, April 21, 1980, p.4.
[3] Charles E. Jefferson, *The Character of Paul* (Macmillan N.Y. 1924) p.32.

Chapter 2

[4] John Pollock, *The Man who Shook the World* (Wheaton, Victor Books 1972) Preface.
[5] Robert E. Speer, *Paul, the All-round Man* (New York, Revell, 1909) p.102.
[6] Frederick B. Meyer, *Paul* (London, Morgan & Scott, 1910) p.34.
[7] *The Character of Paul*, p.19.
[8] J. Oswald Sanders, *Bible Men of Faith* (Chicago, Moody 1966) p.200 ff.
[9] The Sunday School Times, 30 September 1928, p.397.
[10] Clarence Macartney, *The Greatest Men of the Bible* (New York, Abingdon, 1941) p.14.
[11] F. B. Meyer, *Paul*, p.64.

Chapter 3

[12] John R. W. Stott, *God's Men* (Chicago, Inter-Varsity n.d.) p.24.

[13] Robert E. Speer, *The Man Paul* (London, S. W. Partridge n.d.) p.289.

[14] Reginald E. O. White, *Apostle Extraordinary* (London, Pickerings, 1962).

[15] James T. Dyet, *Man of Steel and Man of Velvet* (Denver, Accent Books, 1976) p.55.

[16] Harrington C. Lees, *St. Paul and his Friends* (London, Robert Scott, n.d.) p.11.

[17] *Paul the All-Round Man*, p.124.

[18] Phyllis Thompson, *D. E. Hoste* (London, Lutterworth Press n.d.) p.157.

[19] William Barclay, *Letters of Peter and Jude* (Edinburgh, St. Andrews Press) p.258.

Chapter 4

[20] Alden W. Tozer, *The Knowledge of the Holy* (Harrisburg, Christian Publications, 1961) p.9.

[21] Frank Colquhoun, *Total Christianity* (Chicago, Moody, 1962) p.60.

Chapter 6

[22] Edward M. Bounds, *Prayer and Praying Men* (London, Hodder & Stoughton, 1921) p.109.

[23] Handley C. G. Moule, *Secret Prayer* (London, Marshalls n.d.) p.113.

Chapter 7

[24] Kenneth Gangel, *So you want to be a Leader* (Harrisburg, Christian Publications, 1973) p.14.
[25] Frederick B. Meyer, *Paul*, p.122.
[26] Edward M. Blaiklock, *Bible Characters* (London, Scripture Union, 1974) p.127.

Chapter 8

[27] George W. Peters, *Biblical Theology of Missions* (Chicago, Moody, 1972) p.165.
[28] J. Oswald Sanders, *Bible Men of Faith*, p.219.

Chapter 9

[29] A. T. Robertson, *The Glory of the Ministry* (New York, Revell, 1911) p.59.
[30] Quoted in Robert E. Speer's *Master of the Heart* (New York, Revell, 1908) p.39.
[31] *Paul the All-round Man*, p.65.
[32] *Apostle Extraordinary*, p.62.
[33] *The Man Paul*, p.107.
[34] A. T. Robertson, *Word Pictures of New Testament* (New York, Harpers, 1930) p.248.
[35] Henry F. Rall, *According to Paul* (New York, Scribers 1944) p.215.
[36] *The Greatest Men of the Bible*, p.18.

Chapter 10

[37] Don Williams, *Paul and Women in the Church* (Glendale, Gospel Light, 1977) p.11.
[38] *The Man Paul*, p.104.
[39] *Evangelicals and the Ordination of Women* (Kent, Grove Books 1973) p.24.
[40] *Paul and Women in the Church* p.112.
[41] *Evangelicals and the Ordination of Women*, p.21.
[42] Sanday and Headlam, *The Epistle to the Romans* (Edinburgh, T. & T. Clark, 1902) p.423.
[43] *Evangelicals and the Ordination of Women*, p.25.

Chapter 11

[44] James S. Stewart, *Thine is the Kingdom* (Edinburgh St. Andrews Press) p.23.
[45] A. T. Robertson, *The Glory of the Ministry* (New York, Revell 1911) p.253.
[46] Ibid. p.24
[47] James Denney, *Expositors Bible: Corinthians* (London, Hodder & Stoughton) p.160.

Index of Persons

Scripture Index